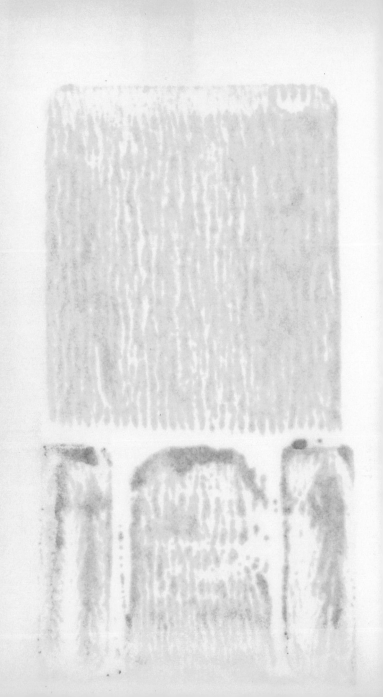

THE COMMONWEALTH AND INTERNATIONAL LIBRARY

PERGAMON OXFORD RUSSIAN SERIES

GENERAL EDITOR: C. V. JAMES

TEACHING AIDS: VOLUME 7

ASPECTIVAL USAGE
IN RUSSIAN

ASPECTIVAL USAGE IN RUSSIAN

A. B. MURPHY

Senior Lecturer,
Royal Military Academy, Sandhurst

PERGAMON PRESS

OXFORD · LONDON · EDINBURGH · NEW YORK
PARIS · FRANKFURT

Pergamon Press Ltd., Headington Hill Hall, Oxford
4 & 5 Fitzroy Square, London W.1

Pergamon Press (Scotland) Ltd., 2 & 3 Teviot Place, Edinburgh 1

Pergamon Press Inc., 122 East 55th St., New York 22, N.Y.

Pergamon Press GmbH, Kaiserstrasse 75, Frankfurt-am-Main

Federal Publications Ltd., Times House, River Valley Rd., Singapore

Samcax Book Services Ltd., Queensway, P.O. Box 2720, Nairobi, Kenya

First edition 1965

Library of Congress Catalog Card No. 64–66364

Printed in Germany

Contents

Оглавление

ГЛАВА IV — ПОВЕЛИТЕЛЬНОЕ НАКЛОНЕНИЕ

ГЛАВА V — ИНФИНИТИВ

Preface

ʜɪs book does not set out to give a complete description of the
ɪpects of the Russian verb. The morphology of the verb is treated
ore than adequately in several Russian works on the subject,
ɪme of which are listed in our bibliography. For this reason the
ɪtroduction in particular is only an outline of the main points
 be considered. The chapters which follow are an attempt to
ovide some guidance on the reasons governing the choice of the
ɪrfective or imperfective in various cases, a point which many non-
ɪtive students of Russian find difficult to grasp, though the native
ɪes it as a matter of course and often cannot understand why we
ɪuld make mistakes. The examples have been drawn from Soviet
ɪthors or from conversations in everyday life. Translations are
ɪod generally only for the cases given, and for further meanings
ɪictionary should be consulted.

Aspects are subject to tendencies rather than rules: if educated
ɪakers favour a certain aspect in a given situation nine times out
 ten (e.g. the imperfective after the negative in the past), that is
ɪat I have taken to be the normal usage. In the minority of cases
ɪere the other aspect is used, there are generally special reasons for
ɪnd these are shown wherever possible.

 am greatly indebted to my supervisor, Professor P. S. Kuzne-
ɪv, for the time and trouble he took in reading the first draft of the
ɪious chapters. Professor O. S. Akhmanova also saw the work
ɪn early stage and made many useful suggestions for improve-
ɪnt. I would like to thank besides M. Wheeler, Esq., M. J. F.
ɪncan, Esq. and M. Davydov, who provided much help on

points of detail, and I am especially grateful to my teachers
Moscow State University: A. N. Vassileva and I. P. Slesarev
who were always prepared to give advice and encouragement.

R.M.A, Sandhurst, 1962. A.B.M

Abbreviations

arch. — archaic
cf. — compare
conv. — conversational
fem. — feminine
freq. — frequentative
impf. — imperfective
instr. — instrumental
lit. — literally
masc. — masculine
perf. — perfective
pop. — popular

Introduction

A. THE CONTRAST BETWEEN THE ENGLISH AND RUSSIAN VERBAL SYSTEMS

The fact that aspectival usage in Russian may appear to be such
thorny subject can be partially explained by the comparative
aucity of tenses in this language. Students will be familiar with
e normal pattern of the Russian verb:

	Imperfective		Perfective	
uture	я бу́ду получа́ть	*I shall be receiving* (*I shall receive*)	я получу́	*I shall receive*
esent	я получа́ю	*I receive, am receiving, do receive*		
ast	я получа́л	*I was receiving* (*I received*)	я получи́л	*I received* (*I have received*)

The translation of the above verbal forms is purely conventional,
d many other renderings might be found, depending on the con-
t in which the verb is placed. This will be obvious if one examines
e multiplicity of English tense forms and realises that all the shades
meaning represented by them must find an equivalent in Russian
der one of the five forms in the above table (it is true that the

forms with the particle бы are not included; they have not been treated separately in the succeeding chapters since it seems to us that the conditional presents few special difficulties with regard to the choice of aspect).

Old Russian was formerly equipped with a more complex structure of tenses, corresponding respectively to the *past continuous* (or imperfect), *the pluperfect*, *the aorist* (or past definite), and the *perfect* (i.e. English form "I have done", etc.).

Of these four forms only the last has survived in modern usage, and it has been stripped of its auxiliary, so that what was formerly a compound tense with auxiliary plus participle (есмь понялъ) now appears as participle alone (я понял). All four of the former meanings have now to be translated by this sole surviving type of past tense, and in fact the perfective (я понял) would normally be used to give three of these meanings, namely: *I have understood* (perfect); *I understood* or *I realised* (aorist); *I had understood* (pluperfect). The imperfective will generally cover the imperfect (*I was understanding*; *used to understand*, etc.) besides other nuances such as *I understood formerly* (*but do not now understand*) etc.

It is as well to be clear from the outset that *no exact correspondence can be sought between English tenses and Russian aspect*, and attempts to find such a correspondence are the source of many mistakes. Some Russian grammarians consider that the English verbal system also contains two main aspects, expressed respectively by the *general* forms ("I write/wrote/will write", etc.) and the *continuous* forms ("I am writing/was writing/will be writing", etc.). However, these divisions also have no real equivalent in the Russian aspectival system and are not of much practical interest for English-speaking students. The *general* aspect is the normal type in English and has a wider range of usage than either of the Russian aspects. Smirnitskii has expressed this clearly in his *Morfologiya angliiskogo yazyka* (see in particular §15 pp. 323–5).

B. SEMELFACTIVES

Modern Russian has preserved only two morphological features which restrict a verb to a specific type of meaning. The most common and important type is that in which the suffix (–ну) is used to express one *single*, completed action. In contrast with this are found a few verbs expressing a repetitive action, with the suffix –ывать/ –ивать, which will be dealt with in the next section of this introduction. In grammatical studies of the last century, verbs with these characteristics were regarded as separate aspectival types (одно- кратный вид, *semelfactive*, and многократный вид, *frequentative*, respectively). They are now listed only as sub-groups of the perfective and imperfective aspects.

The semelfactive verbs end in the suffix –ну– (кри́кнуть, мелькну́ть, сверкну́ть): readers will find them listed in the *Grammatika russkogo yazyka* (Vol. 1, p. 428). It will be noted that all these verbs have no prefix, though in some cases prefixes are added to them to provide additional meanings.

Imperfective	Perfective	
кида́ть	ки́нуть	*to throw*
ки́дывать	ски́нуть	*to throw off*
вига́ть	дви́нуть	*to move* (*trans.*)
ридвига́ть	придви́нуть	*to move something towards oneself, another object*, etc.)

A further feature of these verbs is that they all form their past in the normal way, i.e. by substituting л for the –ть at the end of the infinitive.

Он махну́л руко́й.   *He waved his hand.*

Он нырну́л в во́ду.   *He dived into the water.*

N.B. верну́ться is specifically excluded from this class.

The semelfactives must be distinguished from other verbs ending in –уть which are imperfective when used without a prefix.

Imperfective	Perfective	
тяну́ть	потяну́ть	*to pull*
мо́кнуть	промо́кнуть	*to become wet*
вя́нуть	завя́нуть	*to fade*

Many of this latter class of verbs form short forms of the pas (озя́бнуть/озя́б, исчέзнуть/исчέз), though others have the norma form (верну́ть/верну́л).

Thus in the passage quoted below the verbs in bold type are seme factive with the exception of пови́снуть which means not *to hang (o one occasion)*, but *to be left hanging*. The simple verb скользну́т is regarded as a semelfactive of скользи́ть—*to slip*, but the con pound соскользну́ть is considered the normal perfective of соска́л зывать—*to slip down*.

(1) А морячо́к продолжа́л игра́ть. И дли́нный чуб его́ поло ска́лся по кла́вишам. Пото́м он вдруг опусти́л ру́ки. Он соскользну́ли вниз и **пови́сли**. А голова́ **ткну́лась** в кла́виши, роя́ль и́здал стра́нный гру́стный звук. Все молча́ли. И тогд к моряку́ подошёл офице́р с кра́сной повя́зкой на рукаве́ **козырну́л** и что-то сказа́л. Вдруг все, кто бы́ли бли́же, за рича́ли на офице́ра. (Оку.)

(from infinitives: соскользну́ть, пови́снуть, ткну́ться, козы́ ну́ть).

However the sailor went on playing, and his long forelock swe along the keyboard. Then he suddenly let his hands drop. The slipped down and were left hanging in mid-air. His head struc the keys and the piano gave a strange melancholy sound. Everyor was silent until an officer with a red band on his sleeve came ι to the sailor, saluted and said something. Suddenly all tho who were standing close by began to shout at the officer.

Note that though крича́ть has a semelfactive form, закрича́т is preferred in this instance to convey the meaning: *they began period of shouting.*

C. FREQUENTATIVES

The indeterminate forms of the double imperfective verbs
(ходи́ть, е́здить, бе́гать) are not regarded as frequentatives, since
they must carry the idea of movement "in a number of directions",
quite apart from the habitual action which is characteristic of
frequentative verbs in the conventionally accepted sense. Thus one
would use the indeterminate form in a sentence such as the following:

Бе́гаешь, бе́гаешь весь день и к ве́черу ты совсе́м утомлён.
*You can run (and run) about all day, and by evening you are com-
pletely exhausted.*

However the determinate form will **be** used if the movement is
along a definite course:

Бежи́шь, бежи́шь и, ка́жется, ника́к не доберёшься до до́ма.
You go running on and on, and it seems you will never get home.

The only forms now classed as frequentatives are a few verbs
without prefixes, which contain the suffix –ывать/–ивать. As they
exist mainly as archaisms in popular speech, it is not our intention
to treat them exhaustively. Their frequentative form exists only in
the past and is found alongside the normal form of past tense.

Normal Imperfective	Frequentative	
Он слы́шал (слыха́л)	Он не слы́хивал	*He used not to hear*
Он ви́дел (вида́л)	Он не ви́дывал	*He used not to see*
Он сиде́л	Он си́живал	*He used to sit*

N.B. слы́хивать and ви́дывать are normally used with a negative.

See also: . . . мир об э́том ещё не слы́хивал. (Нил.)
. The world had not yet heard of this.

and: –А я, Салама́тушка, про тебя́ худо́го сло́ва не гова́ривал
и Тимофе́я не ха́ял. (Пер.)

*"But, Salamatushka, I spoke no evil of you and found no fault
with Timofei."*

A number of verbs with the prefix по– also have frequentative forms, e.g.

Он похáживал   *He walked up and down several times*

All the frequentatives mentioned above are really odd survivals in present-day Russian, and even where repetitive action is indicated, it is much more common to find the normal form of past (слы́-шал, ви́дел, сиде́л, говори́л). The only case in which the form is really alive and widely used is the frequentative of быть (*to be*). This is used whenever the speaker wishes to point a contrast between the position at the moment and the normal state of affairs, and, unlike слы́хивать, the verbs быва́ть, похáживать etc. may be used in both the present and the past.

— Скажи́те, у вас есть гóрные лы́жи?
— Нет.
— А они́ у вас **быва́ют**?
— Да, **быва́ют**.
"*Tell me, please, have you got (can I buy) mountain skis?*"
"*No.*"
"*Do you stock them at all?*"
"*Yes, we do have them sometimes.*"
А штóрмы на се́вере Ти́хого океáна пóздней óсенью ре́дко **быва́ют** ме́ньше десяти́ (бáллов). (Кон.)
But in the northern Pacific in late autumn the storms are rarely less than force ten.

D. SECONDARY IMPERFECTIVES

The normal use of the suffix –ыва/–ива/–ва in modern Russian is to form the imperfective aspect of a verb which has acquired a specialised meaning through the addition of a prefix. One might quote such instances *ad infinitum*, as in practice almost any Russian verb with a prefix can form a secondary imperfective in this way. These lengthened imperfectives are normal forms and have n

equentative force (except when the context may require it), i.e.
ney function exactly as other imperfective forms.

Imper- fective (of ori- inal erb)		Per- fective (with prefix giving new meaning)	Secondary imperfective (retaining force of prefix)	
грáть	to play	вы́играть	выи́грывать	to win
исáть	to write	описáть	опи́сывать	to describe
		подписáть	подпи́сывать	to sign
		приписáть	припи́сывать	to ascribe
ть	to beat	уби́ть	убивáть	to kill
		разби́ть	разбивáть	to shatter
		сбить	сбивáть	to beat (eggs, etc.), knock off one's feet etc.
		переби́ть	перебивáть	to interrupt

Пари́ж меня́ учи́л, обогащáл, разоря́л, стáвил нá ноги и
сбивáл с ног. (Э.)

*Paris educated me, enriched me, reduced me to penury, set me
on my feet and knocked me off my feet again.*

—Ты скажи́ — стрáшно на войнé-то — **перебивáла** онá, гля́дя
емý в лицó . . . (Тол.)

*"Tell me, is it frightening when you are at the front?" she would inter-
rupt him, gazing into his face . . ."*

Вáля: . . . А я замёрзла . . . водá, знáешь, дáже льди́нки в
ней. Éле доплылá.

Шýра: . . . А он тут **переживáл**. (Сим.)

*Valya: . . . But I am frozen . . . the water has even got little bits
of ice in it, you know. I have just managed to swim the distance.
Shura: And he was really worried about you here.*

The last quoted dialogue provides an example of a secondar͟y imperfective which is entirely distinct in meaning from the perfec͟tive пережи́ть (to survive). Пережива́ть, when used in this in͟transitive sense, means in fact *to suffer mentally from anxiety o͟r fear* etc. We may say that in this particular meaning пережива́т͟ь has no corresponding perfective.

The addition of a prefix to a simple verb may introduce a com͟paratively slight change in meaning, as for example зако́нчит͟ь which means *to round off* (*a meeting, a speech*, etc.) in contras͟t with конча́ть/ко́нчить (to finish). Nevertheless, when an imper͟fective is called for, an author will prefer to retain this nuanc͟e rather than to revert to the original imperfective.

Во вто́рник собира́лись (шофёры) во дворе́ исполко́ма ͟в у́зком соста́ве, во вре́мя заседа́ний рабо́чего прези́диум͟а, в сре́ду о́коло горко́ма, пока́ **заседа́ло** бюро́, в четве́рг ͟— опя́ть во дворе́ исполко́ма в расши́ренном соста́ве. Зде͟сь **зака́нчивались** все недои́гранные па́ртии, вре́мени хвата́ло ͟— заседа́ние исполко́ма начина́лось в три часа́ и **зака́нчивало͟сь** не ра́ньше десяти́. (Вас.)

On Tuesdays, during the sittings of the Workers' Praesidiu͟m, they would meet in reduced numbers in the courtyard outside t͟he Executive Committee rooms, on Wednesdays by the Town Coun͟cil building, while the administrative staff were in session, and o͟n Thursdays they would meet in full strength—again in the courtya͟rd of the Executive Committee. Here all the unfinished games wer͟e played out—there was plenty of time, as a sitting of the Committe͟e would begin at three o'clock and not finish before ten.

Заседа́ть illustrates another method of forming the secondar͟y imperfective (from the perfective засе́сть) by reverting to the o͟ld stem сед–. Compare several verbs formed from есть (*to eat͟*

Perfective	Secondary Imperfective	
съесть	съеда́ть	*to eat up*
надое́сть	надоеда́ть	*to pester, bore, worry*

The next example shows impfs. from взблесну́ть, etc.

Вечере́ющее со́лнце **взблёскивало** на воде́, листва́ тополе́й на берегу́ почерне́ла от краснова́тых луче́й со́лнца. Бы́ло тепло́, ве́тер, мя́гкий, сла́вный, **проска́льзывал** в коро́ткие рукава́, и блу́зка на груди́ **вздра́гивала**. (Кон.)
The setting sun was glittering on the water and the leaves of the poplars on the bank had become black from the reddish rays. It was warm, and a wonderful, soft breeze, slipping under her short sleeves, was ruffling the inside of her blouse.

Occasionally a secondary imperfective appears to be based on a perfective which has disappeared from the language. Compare formations from гляде́ть (*to look at*):

Perfective	Secondary Imperfective	
погляде́ть	погля́дывать	*to steal glances at (frequentative)*
пригляде́ться	пригля́дываться	*to get accustomed by studying*
загляде́ться	загля́дываться	*to be spellbound*
заглянýть	загля́дывать	*to call on*

загляде́ть does not exist except as a reflexive).

Лёша был возбуждён, реши́телен и ча́сто **погля́дывал** на часы́.
Lyosha was strung up and resolute and stole frequent glances at his watch.

Он нере́дко **загля́дывал** к Сила́нтию Ря́шкину, и Фёдор, **пригля́дываясь** к ним, ника́к не мог поня́ть — друзья́ и́ли враги́ проме́ж собо́й э́ти два челове́ка. (Тен.)
He used quite often to look in on Silantii Ryashkin, and, when he studied them, Fyodor could not make out at all whether these two men were friends or enemies.

E. FORCE OF PREFIXES

If a perfective verb is a true "pair" for the corresponding imperfective, it will contain only the idea of completion or result, and no secondary meanings. Generally speaking all prefixes change the meaning of the verb; in some cases only a slight shift in meaning is felt, in others the change is drastically sharp. It is possible to receive some guidance by examining the force of the various prefixes.

по– and с– are those that are most likely to form perfectives with no additional nuance beyond the completion of the action described by the imperfective. Many pairs of this type come to mind immediately, of which only a few are here listed:

Imperfective	Perfective	
бить	побить	*to beat*
красить	покрасить	*to paint*
вредить	повредить	*to harm*
верить	поверить	*to believe*
весить	повесить	*to hang*
плести	сплести	*to weave*
беречь	сберечь	*to take care of*
гнуть	согнуть	*to bend*
делать	сделать	*to do, make*

(вешать is now used instead of весить).

Used with verbs such as these по– and с– may be called "neutral" prefixes; thus он побил его means simply *he beat him*, without any secondary idea that the process was limited in time or quantity. Even these most neutral of prefixes, however, have a disconcerting habit of taking on quite definite meanings under certain circumstances. по– has frequently the notion of "a little", and with verbs of motion an entirely distinct idea of "starting into movement". Thus он поспал means *he slept for a little*, он поел—*he had a snack*; он побежал means *he began to run*, он пошёл —*he began to walk* etc.

Он **посиде́л, подрема́л, и пошёл** гуля́ть.
He sat for a little, had a snooze, and went off for a walk.
И я рад, что опя́ть **побыва́л** в мо́ре и что пла́вал вме́сте с тобо́й. (Кон.)
And I am glad that I have spent a bit of time at sea again and that I served on the same ship as you.

In contrast it can be seen from the following examples that with, for instance, стара́ться, по– carries no overtone of action limited in extent.

Я постара́юсь привести́ ди́зель в поря́док. Я о́чень **постара́юсь**, Глеб. (Кон.)
I will try and get the diesel engine to work properly. I will try with all my heart and soul, Gleb.
Вообще́ на э́тот раз Лёнька здо́рово **постара́лся**. (Сар.)
Taken all round Lyon'ka had really tried this time.

The prefix c– with verbs of motion has the force of "going down" (он сошёл с трибу́ны—he came down from the platform) and sometimes of "coming together" (им не удаётся свести́ концы́ с конца́ми—they cannot make ends meet). With other verbs c– has simply the meaning of bringing the action in question to a successful conclusion; note its force in the following example:

И, руга́я их, он никогда́ не руга́л челове́ка за то, что тот не **смог**, а всегда́ за то, что тот мог и не **сде́лал**. А е́сли челове́к де́лал мно́гое, то комисса́р ста́вил ему́ в упрёк, что он не **сде́лал** ещё бо́льше. (Сим.)
And when he upbraided them he never abused a man for what he had not managed to do, but always for what he could have done and had not accomplished. Whereas if a man did a great deal, then the Commissar would reproach him with the fact that he had not accomplished even more.

Although it might seem necessary to examine each verb individually, it is in fact possible to deduce general tendencies in the use of prefixes. They are conventionally divided into four groups, ranging from the most neutral to those which always introduce a new shade of meaning in the perfective. The lists of meanings given for each prefix in **Очерки по общей и русской лексикологии,** О. С. Ахманова (pp. 147–50) will be found useful in this context. As this subject is outside the main theme of the present work only a small sample is given.

(1) Neutral prefixes: по–, о–/об–, с–, за–.

Imperfective	Perfective	
шпа́рить	ошпа́рить	*to scald*
пломбирова́ть	запломбирова́ть	*to fill (a tooth)*

по– and с–, as has been quoted above, are the prefixes which most often have a purely neutral meaning. As an example of об– used with neutral force we may quote:

— Запрети́ли их (медве́дей) стреля́ть, вот они́ и **обнагле́ли**, — сказа́л Во́льнов. (Кон.)
"We have been forbidden to shoot them and now they have got really impudent," said Vol'nov.

об– is half-way to being a neutral prefix in the perfective of трепа́ться (to fray):

Он (флаг) совсе́м небольшо́й у нас на се́йнерах и ещё **об-тре́плется** за доро́гу. (Кон.)
We have quite a small flag on our drifters and it will get frayed besides on our journey.

In practice о– has much more frequently its other meanings of *around* etc. (обкопа́ть — *to dig round*, etc.).* It is presumably included in this first group because of the large number of perfectives formed with it from verbs which no longer exist (обману́ть, объясни́ть).

* For a list of these meanings see Грамма́тика ру́сского языка́, том 1, стр. 587–90.

The most widespread use of за– is to form inchoative verbs which describe the beginning of an action (закричáть — *to shout*, заплáкать — *to weep*). Though the literal sense of these verbs is *to start shouting* and *to burst into tears*, they are in fact very close to being simply neutral perfectives for the verbs кричáть and плáкать. It is true that крúкнуть and поплáкать also exist as aspectical pairs for these two verbs, but their use is not always appropriate, as крúкнуть has semelfactive force, and поплáкать implies that the crying is limited in duration. In practice there is little difference in meaning between крúкнуть and закричáть, as will be seen from the following example:

—Кудá вы идёте, там я́ма, **закричáл** он и дёрнул Мúшу за рукáв.
"*Where are you going? There is a hole there,*" *he shouted and tugged Misha's sleeve.*

Закричáл is here a verb with the same force as the semelfactive дёрнул, both of them expressing a single, instantaneous action. In view of cases such as these it seems that закричáть is classified as an inchoative purely for conventional reasons, though it may occasionally have this meaning in certain contexts.

In the case of поплáкать the prefix по– has definitely sometimes an overtone of "a little" or "for a short time". However, the difference between поплáкать and заплáкать is in fact slight.

Онá хотéла **поплáкать,** но плáкать кáк-то нé было охóты, бы́ло прóсто грýстно. (Казв.)
She wanted to have a cry, but somehow she could not bring herself to weep, she just felt sad.

Дýся стáла перебирáть стáрые кáрточки и опя́ть не моглá **заплáкать**: на всех кáрточках у мáтери бы́ло чужóе напряжённое лицó. (Казв.)
Dusya began to look through the old photographs and again she could not cry: in all the photographs her mother's face was unsmiling and seemed to belong to a stranger.

(2) Prefixes which generally alter the sense of the verb: из–, на–. вы–, про–, у–, вз–, от–.

Spagis quotes from this group two examples of the use of на–:

Ты уже **написал** сочинение! Вот хорошо!

You have already written your essay! That's fine!

(на– is "neutral", simply making the verb perfective.)

Он **наклеил** марку на конверт.

He stuck the stamp on the envelope.

(на–, besides making клеить perfective, has the additional meaning of *onto*.)

Similar pairs of contrasting verbs might be quoted for all the prefixes in this second category. Compare, for example, упасть, which is the "neutral" perfective of падать, with the perfective of видеть also formed with у–:

Он **упал** в озеро.

He fell in the lake.

Я **увидел** его на улице вчера.

I caught sight of him in the street yesterday.

(i.e. *I saw him—momentarily—but was not speaking to him.*)

Я **видел** его на улице вчера.

This might mean *I met him* (*and stopped to talk to him*), but it also may mean exactly the same as я увидел его.

Упасть serves падать as a perfective in all cases where it signifies "fall" in the concrete sense.

As an example of the neutral force of от– we find:

Бумага в журнале радиосвязи **отсырела** . . . (Кон.)

The paper in the radio log has got damp . . .

(3) The third group of prefixes almost always introduces another meaning over and above the simple idea of completion of the action:

при–, пере–, раз–/рас–, под–, воз–/вос–/вз–/вс–.

идти́ + при–	прийти́	*to come*
идти́ + пере–	перейти́	*to go across*
идти́ + раз– + сь	разойти́сь	*to disperse, go off in different directions*
идти́ + под–	подойти́	*to approach*
идти́ + вз–	взойти́	*to go up, mount*

More rarely than is the case with the verbs in group 2, these prefixes may occasionally form perfectives which do not differ in meaning from the simple imperfective, e.g. по́льзоваться/воспо́льзоваться, *to make use of*.

(4) Prefixes which invariably force a special meaning in the perfective. The instances where the prefix is close to a neutral meaning are even rarer than those occurring in group 3. With the exception of до– and в–these are the least commonly used of all the verbal prefixes. The list of meanings given in the following table is not intended to be exhaustive, and the reader may consult a dictionary for further meanings.

Imperfective		Perfective	
идти́	*to go* + в–	войти́	*to go into*
идти́	*to go* + до–	дойти́	*to go as far as*
лома́ть	*to break* + над–	надломи́ть	*to fracture (bones), overtax one's strength (formed from ломи́ть a conversational form of лома́ть)*
станов́иться	*to become* + недо–	недоста́ть	*to be lacking (formed from perfective ста́ть)*

Imperfective		Perfective	
класть	*to put* + низ–	низложи́ть	*to depose* (*form-ed from vulgar form* ложи́ть)
цени́ть	*to value* + обез–	обесце́нить	*to cheapen*
сказа́ть	*to say* + пред–	предсказа́ть	*to foretell*
рвать	*to tear* + пре–	прерва́ть	*to interrupt*

Almost all the verbs given in groups 3 and 4 are equipped with fresh imperfectives which retain the new meaning introduced by the prefix:

Imperfective	Perfective
3. приходи́ть, переходи́ть	прийти́, перейти́
расходи́ться	разойти́сь
подходи́ть, всходи́ть	подойти́, взойти́
4. доходи́ть	дойти́
надла́мывать	надломи́ть
недостава́ть	недоста́ть
низлага́ть	низложи́ть
обесце́нивать	обесце́нить
предска́зывать	предсказа́ть
прерыва́ть	прерва́ть

The *Grammatika russkogo yazyka* regards –ать as an alternative suffix for forming secondary imperfectives in certain cases, and states that, though less productive of new verbs than the –ыв– –ив– suffix, it is still used in certain cases, particularly after stems ending in a sibilant (сообща́ть/сообщи́ть etc.).

Dictionaries will, of course, show these "secondary" imper fectives as the true aspectual pairs, and considerations of thi nature have led Ushakov, for example, to regard the perfective a the dominant form of the verb and to list it primarily, with th imperfective as a mere adjunct. Isachenko has tended to regar all formations with prefixes as differing in meaning from the original imperfective; he regards only verbs of the type открыва́ть/откры́ть as true aspectival pairs. For the student of the language, however, it is a widely accepted convention to list the imperfective as the primary form in vocabularies and dictionaries, and it also provides a useful working basis to regard verbs such as де́лать/сде́лать as the imperfective and perfective of one and the same verb. It should, however, be borne in mind that any prefix may alter the meaning of the verb to such an extent that the perfective will express a completely new conception.

F. TRANSITIVE AND INTRANSITIVE VERBS

A verb which is only transitive in one aspect may sometimes have both transitive and intransitive meanings in the other. Generally it is the imperfective which embraces the wider range of meanings. пережи́ть, for instance, can be only transitive, with the sense either (1) *to survive*:

Он **пе́режил** Чайко́вского на де́сять лет.
He survived Chaikovskii by ten years.
Он пе́режил свои́ жела́ния.
He outlived his hopes and ambitions.

or (2) *to live through, to experience*:

Он мно́го **пе́режил** во вре́мя войны́.
He had a bad time during the war.

The corresponding imperfective can express both these meanings.

Жёны ча́сто **пережива́ют** свои́х муже́й.

(1) *Wives often survive their husbands.*
Он **пережива́л** мно́го тру́дностей на рабо́те.

(2) *He was experiencing many difficulties at his work.*

With the imperfective the latter meaning has been extended to cover also cases where there is no direct object, in the sense of *to take to heart, to suffer* (*mentally*).

Не на́до так **пережива́ть**.
You should not get so worked up.
Она́ о́чень **пережива́ет**.
She is suffering greatly.

This usage of the verb пережива́ть is comparatively new, but it has now been widely accepted and is used in colloquial speech.

A few of the most common imperfective verbs in Russian have in fact two separate functions: (1) intransitive, simply describing the action (I read, I write, I see), and (2) transitive (I often read poetry, I write many letters, I see a dark object).

Intransitive	Transitive
— Что ты де́лаешь?	— Что ты чита́ешь?
— Я **чита́ю**.	— Я **чита́ю** «Ти́хий Дон».
"*What are you doing?*"	"*What are you reading?*"
"*I am reading.*"	"*I am reading 'Quiet Flows the Don'.*"
Этот ребёнок не уме́ет **писа́ть**.	Он **пи́шет** сочине́ние.
This child cannot write.	*He is writing an essay.*
Слепо́й **бу́дет ви́деть**.	Он **ви́дит** чёрное о́блако.
The blind man will see.	*He sees a black cloud.*

The perfectives прочита́ть, написа́ть, уви́деть are pairs only to the second of these meanings and require an object either real or implied.

G. DIFFERENCE IN MEANING
BETWEEN APPARENT PAIRS

Depending on the context in which they are used, verbs which are conventionally regarded as pairs may be translated by separate and distinct words in English.

Imperfective		Perfective	
говори́ть	*to speak*	сказа́ть	*to say*
убежда́ть	*to persuade*	убеди́ть	*to convince*
объясня́ться	*to listen to each other's point of view*	объясни́ться	*to arrive at an understanding*

e.g. Дава́йте **объясни́мся** . . .   *Let's get this straight . . .*

H. NEW FORMATIONS

Individual Russians are quite ready to use a new verbal form in cases where they feel that a specific situation demands a shade of meaning not covered by one of the forms already in existence. If the need for the new aspect is felt to be permanent and widespread it will rapidly come to be accepted as an established usage. These neologisms can only be used with reserve by foreign students of Russian, and it is usually advisable to consult a good dictionary which gives some indication of the "colour" of the word in question. The new verbal formations are of three types:

(1) Fresh imperfectives formed from perfectives containing prefixes by the addition of the suffix –ывать/–ивать.

— Я хоте́ла немно́го перекуси́ть в буфе́те.
— А я соверше́нно не собира́лась сейча́с **перекѵ́сывать**.
"I wanted to have something to eat in the buffet."
"But I had no intention of eating anything at present."
Это случи́лось как раз когда́ наш косми́ческий кора́бль **прилу́нивался**.
This happened just at the time when our space ship was landing on the moon.

(2) Semelfactive perfectives with suffix –ну.

Когда́ ты бу́дешь в Москве́, мы хорошо́ **гульнём** (*pop.*) вме́сте.
When you come to Moscow we will have a good time together.

There are also some semelfactives formed with the suffix –ану–. These are almost invariably popular usage, and are found mainly in the countryside.

—А своё судно́ я ещё не при́нял с заво́да, и **долбану́л** тебя́. (Кон.)

"*But I still have not taken over my ship from the yard and I have been in collision with you.*"

(3) Perfectives formed with a prefix not previously applied to the verb in question. A perfective form of рабо́тать with the prefix c– has long existed as a popular usage in the sense of *to manufacture*.

Он **срабо́тал** па́ру боти́нок.

He knocked up a pair of shoes.

With the coming of automatic machines the need was felt for a perfective to express the idea that the machine carried out the operation it was designed to perform.

Маши́на продвига́лась вперёд, педа́ль **срабо́тала** и светофо́р показа́л зелёный свет.

The car moved forward, the traffic mat acted and the lights changed from red to green.

This meaning of the verb has had sufficiently wide currency for it now to be accepted as normal also in the written language.

. . . они́ с тра́лений в Кроншта́дт. **Срабо́тала** до́нная акусти́-ческая ми́на. (Кон.)

They were coming to Kronstadt from trawling operations. An acoustic mine on the bottom went off.

И тут **срабо́тала** его́ проница́тельность. От тишины́, цари́в-шей в до́ме, от таи́нственного шо́роха в ко́мнате до́чери, Христофо́рову ста́ло не по себе́. (Вас.)

And at this point his perceptive powers came into play. Khristo-forov was overcome by a feeling of uneasiness when he noticed the stillness of the house and the mysterious rustling sounds coming from his daughter's room.

In modern dictionaries no verb is given to correspond to the noun пылесóс (*vacuum cleaner*). Yet in conversational usage not only has such a verb been formed, but it has also been equipped with a perfective, so that one may commonly hear sentences such as:

Я **пропылесóсила** девя́тый эта́ж.
I have cleaned the ninth floor with a vacuum cleaner.

I. CONCLUSION

Lastly it should be stressed again that the concept of "aspect" is not synonymous with that of "tense," and that in many sentences one aspect may be substituted for the other with only a slight change in emphasis. On this subject it seems appropriate to close the introduction with the following quotation from Isachenko:

"Where the imperfective aspect is used to express the idea of an action in progress (for example я перепи́сывал/я перепи́сываю) the speaker is as it were himself fully immersed in the current of this process. He can see neither the beginning nor the end of it and hence is unable to express the process as a completed action seen as a complete entity. His position may be compared to that of a man marching in the May Day Parade who is moving along with the mass of the people and can see neither the beginning nor the end of the procession.

Where the action is expressed by forms of the perfective aspect (for example я переписа́л), the speaker is standing outside the action expressed by the verbal form and therefore surveys the action as one whole. The speaker is now viewing the action from the point of view of those who stand on the platform during the parade and who can see both the beginning and the end of the procession, so that the parade gives them an impression which is complete in itself." (Isachenko, pp. 132–3.)

I. Past Tenses

A. IMPERFECTIVE ASPECT

(1) Repetitive Action

(a) Repeated Action Proper

In the most obvious cases the choice of the imperfective aspect will be suggested by an adverb:

Такую рыбу мы **редко** ловили.
This was a sort of fish that we rarely caught.

or an adverbial phrase:

В сумерках мы **то и дело** попадали в сугробы.
In the twilight we got into snowdrifts every so often.

Я **много раз** просил об этом товарища командира, но он не разрешал. (Сим.)
I made this request to the Commander many times, but he would not give me permission.

If the idea of repeated or habitual action were not dominant in these sentences, the verb would stand in the perfective.

Мы **поймали** такую рыбу (раз).
We caught this sort of fish (once).

Мы **попали** в сугроб.
We got into a snowdrift.

Я **попросил** об этом товарища командира, но он не разрешил.
I asked the Commander about this, but he did not give me permission.

Expressions such as ча́сто, ре́дко will demand an imperfective even where the verb is well separated from the adverb or adverbial phrase. In the example which follows, the adverbial phrase не́сколько раз necessitates the use of the imperfective предлага́ли, and this in its turn means that отка́зывался must also be imperfective, being an action which occurred explicitly "several times."

Ему́ **не́сколько раз** предлага́ли бо́лее кру́пные до́лжности, сва́тали да́же в замести́тели председа́теля горпромсове́та, но он, по́мня о свое́й бу́рной биогра́фии и о не́котором несоотве́тствии анке́тных да́нных с жите́йской пра́ктикой, ве́жливо, но твёрдо **отка́зывался**. (Вас.)

Several times more important posts were offered to him, and they even attempted to get him in as a Deputy Chairman of the Urban Industrial Council; however, remembering his stormy life history and certain discrepancies between his actual record and that shown on his documents, he politely but firmly refused.

Во́зле перекрёстков он **остана́вливался**, чита́л назва́ние у́лицы и **шёл** да́льше уве́ренным и ро́вным ша́гом. (Казч.)

At the cross-roads he would stop to read a street name, and then go on with an assured and even step.

In this context the determinative form шёл is the only one possible. Ходи́л да́льше could not be used, as it would have the distinct meaning of "going further (than someone else)."

Я ходи́л в шко́лу в село́ Ива́новку за пять киломе́тров от на́шего села́. Пётр **ходи́л** да́льше, в Иванте́евку, так как в Ива́новке десятиле́тки не́ было.

I went to school in the village of Ivanovka which was five kilometres from our village. Pyotr went on further to Ivanteyevka, as there was no ten-year school in Ivanovka.

The following sentence is an interesting case where, by using the perfective of брать, the author has indicated the idea of repeated action with a number of separate animals.

Опанас Кондратыч **брал** щенка за шиворот, **клал** на землю, придавив щёпкой, осторожно **обливал** кипятком из ковша. (Кож.)

Opanas Kondratych took (each) puppy by the scruff of the neck, laid it on the ground and, holding it down with a sliver of wood, carefully scalded it all over with boiling water from the ladle.

An adverb of manner such as осторожно would in any case entail the use of the imperfective aspect обливал even if there were no idea of repetition. An operation which is carried out "slowly" (медленно), or "at length" (долго) is almost inevitably a type of "continuous action", as examined in the next section.

On the other hand adverbs such as "suddenly" (вдруг) which explicitly convey the idea of instantaneous action are found normally with perfective verbs. Note, however, that the concept of "repetition" is strong enough to force the use of the imperfective after вдруг in the following extract, which describes a journey out of Moscow by train.

А потом всё пошло быстрее, трах-тах, тах-тах, трах-тах, тах-тах ... То вдруг **открывалась** дальняя перспектив Москвы, то окно закрывалось вагонами, стоящими н путях, заборами, пакгаузами. (Акс.)

And then everything started to move faster and faster etc. ... At one moment a distant view of Moscow would be opened up, and then the view from the window would be blocked by carriage standing on the rails, or by fences and warehouses.

(b) Habitual Action

Sometimes the frequentative бывало is used to introduce habitual action in the past.

... иногда я работал дни напролёт, исправлял, писал заново, **бывало** — бросал начатое. (Э.)

. . . sometimes I used to work for days at a stretch: I would intro-
duce corrections, write a fresh version, and sometimes give up the
piece that I had begun.

The present tense is also found, and in this case быва́ло is
sufficient to indicate that the action took place in the past.

А он, **быва́ло**, сиди́т и разгова́ривает с на́ми . . .
He used to sit and talk with us . . .

Other adverbial expressions of the same sort also make a clear
demand for the imperfective.

Во вся́кое вре́мя го́да и днём и но́чью **приходи́лось** мне
е́здить на ста́нцию из своего́ села́ и́ли, наоборо́т, в село́ со
ста́нции. (Сол.)
In every season of the year, both by day and by night, I have had to
make the journey to the station from my village, or vice versa to
the village from the station.

Even if no adverbs indicating repetition are included, the
simple fact that the verbs are in the imperfective is by itself sufficient
to show that the actions in question were habitual.

В око́пах шла окая́нная и всё же бу́дничная жизнь: **жда́ли**
по́чты, **дави́ли** вшей, **руга́ли** офице́ров, **расска́зывали** поха́б-
ные анекдо́ты: пото́м **умира́ли**. (Э.)
In the trenches an accursed and yet humdrum life went on: they
waited for the post, squashed lice, abused their officers, told
dirty jokes—then died.

(2) Continuous Action and State of Rest

(a) Action in Progress

The concept of continuous action cannot always be separated
cleanly from that of repetition. The following passage is clearly
marked as continuous by the introductory expression *everything had*
been hung up in the yard.

Всё э́то добро́ бы́ло разве́шено во дворе́, и Стёша, в ста́рень-
ком пла́тьице, из кото́рого выпира́ло её молодо́е, упру́гое
те́ло, приде́рживая одно́й руко́й полуша́лок на плеча́х, с
па́лкой в друго́й, аза́ртно **выбива́ла** залежа́вшуюся пыль и
таба́чный дух. Алевти́на Ива́новна, тёща Фёдора, **помога́ла**
ей. (Тен.)

*All this stuff (clothes) had been hung up in the yard, and Styosha in
an old dress which was taut on her supple, young body, holding her
shawl on her shoulders with one hand, wielded a stick lustily with
the other to beat out the ingrained dust and smell of stale tobacco.
Alevtina Ivanovna, Fyodor's mother-in-law was helping, her.*

Expressions of time using the accusative case without a preposition are generally found with imperfective verbs.

Он **писа́л** кни́гу три го́да.
He had been writing the book for three years.

Only with verbs formed with the prefix про– is it possible to
use a perfective for a simple extent of time.

Я три го́да **рабо́тал**, как негр на планта́ции. (Акс.)
I had been working for three years like a nigger on a plantation.

прорабо́тал might here be substituted without any substantial
change in meaning.

Sentences of this type should be contrasted with those where
за + the accusative is used to express a given period of time within
which an action was completed. With the preposition за used in
this sense the perfective aspect must be used.

За три го́да он **написа́л** кни́гу.
In three years he finished writing the book.

The expression в тече́ние ... which means virtually the same
thing can be used with either aspect, and no more is meant by a
change in aspects than the traditional opposition between "result"
and "process".

В течéние двух лет он **писáл/написáл** кнíгу.
He wrote the book in the course of two years.

Similarly with expressions containing the preposition на +
ccusative, where the verb is in the past it will normally stand in the
erfective.

Он **уéхал** на три гóда/навсегдá и т.п.
He went away for three years/for ever, etc.

The imperfective will be used wherever the feeling of action in
rogress is more important than the result obtained.

– . . . Пусть бы у нас до утрá **оставáлся**.
"*. . . Why could he not stay with us till the morning?*"
Он ждал, когдá же наконéц кóнчится. Но почемý-то не
уходíл — **сидéл и смотрéл.** (Нек.)
*He was waiting for it to come finally to an end. But for some
reason he would not go away, he just sat and watched.*

A continuous action is often expressed by a simple past inde-
nite in English.

Когдá Кузьмá Егóрович чéрез полчасá **покидáл** предéлы
горпромсовéта, егó провожáл тóлько завéдующий произ-
вóдственным отдéлом Любáшин, тóже стрáстный фото-
любíтель. (Вас.)
*Half an hour later when Kuz'ma Yegorovich left the precincts of
the Urban Industrial Council, he was accompanied only by
Lyubashin, manager of the Production Division and like him a
passionate amateur photographer.*

A good example of simultaneous actions viewed under two con-
asting aspects is provided by the following sentence:

Пóсле зáвтрака Мáша бы́стро **убралá** посýду, а Сергéй **помо-
гáл** ей. (S. Khavronina, *Practical Russian*, Moscow, 1962.)
*After breakfast Masha quickly cleared (perf.) the table and Sergei
helped (impf.) her.*

Here the action is visualised and described to the reader as i
takes place rather than regarded as part of a past narrative.

In selecting the aspect in Russian in sentences such as this the
decisive factor is whether stress is to be laid on the action itself o
on its end product. This question will be more fully examined in
section 4 of this chapter.

In common with most European languages Russian uses the
present tense to express a process with its origin in the past which i
still effective at the moment of speaking. In this case English use
the present perfect, either in its continuous form:

Вы давно́ меня́ **ждёте**?
Have you been waiting long for me?

or in the non-continuous form:

Я **живу́** в э́том до́ме 40 лет.
I have lived in this house for forty years.

At one remove further back in the past the Russian imperfectiv
past is similarly used to correspond to an English pluperfect.

С неде́лю **стоя́ла** о́ттепель. (Тен.)
The thaw had been going on for about a week.

Contrast this example with a similar sentence in the perfectiv
aspect:

С неде́лю **простоя́ла** о́ттепель.

Here the action is regarded as completed, the implication bein
either "everything had thawed out" or that "frosts started to
come back".

(b) State of Rest and Scenic Description

Naturally the imperfective is used for scenic descriptions.

У́тренняя се́рость постепе́нно, но с ка́ждой мину́той вс
напо́ристее и быстре́е **вполза́ла** во все ще́ли, **проника́ла**

тёмные подворóтни, **слúзывала** густы́е тéни с порóгов и стен. (Казч.)

Gradually, but with ever growing speed and insistence the grey light of morning crawled into every crack, pushed itself into dark gateways and licked the thick shadows from the doorways and walls.

Тýчи **покрывáли** всё нéбо, но на горизóнте былá протя́нута широ́кая жёлтая полосá. Онá освещáла мóре. Вóлны **перекáтывались** дáльше, слóвно какúе-то ю́ркие тýши под целлофáном. (Акс.)

Storm clouds covered the whole sky except for a broad yellow band along the horizon which lit up the sea. The waves were rolling by like some kind of live bodies moving under cellophane.

Дерéвья **лежáли** поперёк ручья́, образýя лáвы рáзной высоты́, а вы́сохшие вéтви дерéвьев то **касáлись** воды́, то **повисáли** в вóздухе, не доставáя дна буерáка. (Сол.)

The trees lay across the stream, forming a series of layers (lit. lava at various heights), while their dead branches touched the water in places and elsewhere hung in the air without reaching to the bottom of the gully.

The imperfective aspect in descriptions serves as a background against which the narrative actions will be placed in the perctive.

Но э́тому не суждено́ бы́ло сбы́ться. Когдá чéрез мéсяц мы **уезжáли** из Синегóрии, я **забы́л** брóсить монéту. (Наг.)
But this was not fated to come to pass. When we left Sinegoriya a month later I forgot to drop the coin.

) Uncompleted Action

A further type of usage where the imperfective sense stands out ite clearly consists of those sentences where an action has not en brought to a successful conclusion.

(a) Attempted Action

In the most obvious cases a perfective will be contrasted with th
imperfective.

— Меня **убива́ли,** да не **уби́ли,** вот почему́ я здесь. (Тол.)
They tried to kill me, but failed to do so, that is why I am here.

Я до́лго убежда́л преподава́тельницу, что в э́том нет ника
ко́го анархи́зма, наоборо́т. **Убежда́л,** но не **убеди́л.** (Э.)
*For a long time I tried to convince the teacher that this was no
a case of anarchism, but rather the reverse. I argued and argued
but could not convince her.*

В то вре́мя, как она́ говори́ла, Слепцо́в мо́лча **надева́л** н
себя́ шине́ль и ника́к не мог **наде́ть.** (Казч.)
*While she was speaking Sleptsov, without saying a word, wa
trying to put on his greatcoat and simply could not manage to ge
into it.*

Though sometimes an aspectival pair may not be used the ide
of unsuccessful action is still clearly present.

Но как ни **кида́лись** псы, как ни **натя́гивали** про́волоку, он
не могли́ нас доста́ть. (Ол.)
*But no matter how much the dogs hurled themselves at us, n
matter how much they strained at the wire, they could not reach u*

Нача́льник уча́стка **угова́ривал** его́ (Бычко́ва) пойти́ отдо
ну́ть: общежи́тие тут ря́дом с ба́зой, грузовико́м займёт
дежу́рный шофёр. Но Бычко́в не стал его́ слу́шать: не с
и не о́тдых бы́ли ему́ нужны́ сейча́с. (Наг.)
*The head of the section tried to persuade him to go and res
the hostel was right beside the garage and the duty driver wou
look after the lorry. But Bychkov would not listen to him: it was n
sleep or rest that he needed now.*

Шали́н до́лго **вразумля́л** Андриа́нова. Во́вка (Андриа́но
ухмыля́лся. Шали́н по́нял, что не **вразуми́л.** (Гла.)

Shalin for a long time tried to make Andrianov see reason. Vovka grinned. Shalin realised that he had not convinced him.

Гéцке прорывáлся к ворóтам, оставля́я позади́ всех нáших бéков, присéвших от егó быстроты́ и нáтиска на кóрточки, и **ударя́л** в ворóта.

. . . Но Волóдя Макáров, вратáрь совéтской команды, **словил** мяч. (Ол.)

Getske came breaking through towards the goal, leaving all our backs behind him flabbergasted by his speed and impetuosity, and he made a shot at the goal . . . But Volodya Makarov, the Soviet goalkeeper, caught the ball.

(присéсть на кóрточки: lit. *to sit on one's haunches*.)

The idea that "no conscious effort was made" is implicit in the following example.

Я ни о чём **не вспоминáл**, но всё равнó возникáла Гáля. (Акс.)
I was not trying to remember anything in particular, but all the same I kept thinking of Galya.

(возникáть/возни́кнуть: *to rise up; appear*.)

In some instances the idea that the action has been without a successful result is merely implicit.

Сафóнов (Глóбе): Ну, что ты бýдешь дéлать? Как назнáчил егó начáльником осóбого отдéла, так он всё покáзывает лю́дям, что не бои́тся. А э́то, мéжду прóчим, все и так знáют.
Вáля: Я егó **удéрживала, удéрживала.**
Сафóнов: Уж молчи́! Удéрживала онá. Я знáю, как ты удéрживаешь. Самá лéзет не знáю кудá, потóм расскáзывает — **удéрживала** онá! (Сим.)

Safonov (to Globa): Well, what can you do about it? As soon as I've appointed him head of the special section he starts showing the men all the time that he is not afraid. And that is something they all know in any case.

Valya: I tried to hold him back, I tried.
Safonov: You be quiet. She tried to hold him back! I know the
way you try to restrain people. She gets into every kind of danger-
ous spot herself and then tells us that she tried to hold him back.

Such constructions should only be imitated with caution when
translating into Russian; it will normally be necessary to use a
verb "to try" plus an infinitive.

(b) Interrupted Action

Often one action in the imperfective is interrupted by another
in the perfective.

Я **шёл** по пло́щади Клиши́ и **сочиня́л** стихи́, когда́ вдруг
пло́щадь **напо́лнилась** толпо́й. (Э.)
I was walking across the Place Clichy and making up some verse
when suddenly the square filled up with people.

Пото́м я всё вре́мя **шёл** по го́роду, пока́ не попа́л сюда́.
(Акс.)
Then I kept on walking through the town until finally I landed up here.

(c) Action "Done and Undone"

In this section the imperfective is used to describe an action which
has in fact been completed, but which is no longer felt to be effective in the present. Compare the following pairs of sentences:

Imperfective	Perfective
(expressing "result of action destroyed")	(expressing action "still alive in the present")
Он **брал** э́ту кни́гу в библиоте́ке.	Он **взял** э́ту кни́гу в библиоте́ке.
He got that book out of the library (and has given it back).	*He has got that book out of the library (and still has it).*

The use of the perfective aspect as in the second column will be
further examined in the section "Perfective with Result in the

resent". The contrast between perfectives and imperfectives in
his sense is particularly frequently found with verbs of motion.

Imperfective	Perfective
К вам **приходи́л** това́рищ. *A friend has been to see you* (*and went away again*).	К вам **пришёл** това́рищ. *A friend has come to see you* (*and is still there*).
Ко мне **приезжа́ла** сестра́. *My sister has been to visit me* *and has now gone away* *again*).	Ко мне **прие́хала** сестра́. *My sister has come to stay with me* (*and is still there*).
Ко́ля не **приходи́л** без нас? *Did Kolya come in while we* *were out?*	Ко́ля не **пришёл** ещё? *Has Kolya not come yet?*

If imperfectives occur in this meaning in a narrative which is
placed in the past they will normally be translated by an English
pluperfect.

В их отсу́тствие кто́-то **входи́л,** взлома́в дверно́й замо́к;
а уходя́, прила́дил вися́чий. (Пан.)
While they were not there someone had come in by breaking open
the lock on the door, and had fixed a padlock to it on leaving.

Note the use of the perfective in the second half of the proposi-
tion to express the idea "the padlock was still there".

As an extension of the idea of "result destroyed in the present"
we may note cases where it is not clear what has been the result
of a given action and the verb is once more placed in the imperfective to give a note of "vagueness".

Отту́да **переплыва́л** челове́к . . . (Сим.)
A man swam across (*from the other side of the lagoon*).
Здесь кто́-то **подплыва́л** к бе́регу . . . (Сим.)
Someone swam in to the bank here . . .

In both these cases the Russian soldiers who are on guard ar
not certain of the whereabouts of the unknown swimmer at th
moment of speaking: he may have swum away again or he ma
be hiding on their side of the lagoon.

(d) Negative Sentences

As a negative necessarily implies that the action in questio
has not been completed there is a strong tendency to use the im
perfective forms, especially of the past tense and the imperative.

> Она́ ничего́ не **отвеча́ла,** то́лько и́зредка встря́хивала голо
> во́й. (Наг.)
> *She made no reply, but only shook her head from time to tim*
> Каблуко́в интере́са к бесе́де не **проявля́л.** (Вас.)
> *Kablukov showed on interest in the conversation.*

In many cases of course the perfective can also be used in neg
tive sentences. Its general effect will be to add further definition
the idea expressed or to confine it to a definite set of circumstance

Imperfective	Perfective
— Вы получи́ли письмо́?	— Вы получи́ли письмо́?
— Нет, не **получа́л.**	— Нет, я не **получи́л** письмо́ от бра́та.
" Did you get a letter?"	*" Did you get the letter?"*
" No, I did not get one."	*" No, I did not get the letter fr my brother."*
— Вы не встреча́ли её в институ́те?	А я не **встре́тил** его́ на вокза́. так как опозда́л.
— Нет, не **встреча́л.**	
" Did you never run across her at the Institute?"	*I did not manage to meet him at the station because I was late.*
" No, I have not met her."	

Imperfective	Perfective
	— Вы там с ним ра́зве не **встре́тились**, как усла́вливались? "*Did you not manage to meet him there as you had agreed?*"

In the cases where the perfective встре́тить is used with a negative it is, of course, not essential to translate "managed to" in each individual context, but there is generally some implication that some arrangement has gone wrong, and that the meeting has not taken place as planned. In practice unless some such nuance is intended the imperfective встреча́ть is almost always used when a negative occurs in the sentence.

— . . . А Колды́бина ра́зве в Москве́ не встреча́ете? Он там уже́ го́да два. Где́-то отде́л кри́тики возглавля́ет.
— Не **встреча́л**. (Вас.)

"*And do you really never meet Koldybin in Moscow? He has been there about two years now. He is the head of some department of criticism or other.*"

"*I have not met him.*"

Note the switch of aspects in the following extract:

Как то́лько теле́га вы́ехала из заводски́х воро́т, Тётя Уля приказа́ла:
— На Ме́льничную!

На Ме́льничной жила́ её ста́ршая сестра́.

Ку́чер для поря́дка **возрази́л**:
— Сказа́ли на Со́лнечную!

— Ма́ло ли что! Мне видне́е! Дава́й, газу́й!

Ку́чер не **возража́л**, тем бо́лее что сам жил на Ме́льничной. (Вас.)

As soon as the wagon had left the factory gates old Ulya commanded:

"*Drive to Mel'nichnaya Street!*"

Her elder sister lived on Mel'nichnaya Street.
The driver objected for the sake of form: "But they told us to g
to Solnechnaya Street!"
"They're always saying things! I know best! Come on, ste
on it."
The driver made no more objections, all the more so as he himse
lived in Mel'nichnaya Street.

In the case of this particular verb the imperfective возража́т
has simply the sense of "to express an objection", whereas th
perfective возрази́ть requires the sense to be completed, either b
quoting the actual words used, as here, or by a direct object.
would be possible for example to say Он ничего́ не возрази́
though the imperfective is used in the majority of negative sentence
in the past.

The case for the use of the imperfective is particularly strong
sentences where the lack of action is extended over an indefini
period of time.

Впро́чем, я не совсе́м прав, говоря́ что к э́тому просёл
во́все не **притра́гивалась** рука́ челове́ка. (Сол.)
However I am not completely right in saying that this count
road was never touched by the hand of man.

In many negative sentences there is an underlying notion
"did not want to", rather akin to the sentences containing t
idea "tried/did not try" which have already been noted above.

А я не **прова́ливалась,** е́сли хо́чешь знать, — шёпчет Га́лł
— Я и не **поступа́ла,** так и знай. (Акс.)
"I never failed (the examination) if you want to know," whispe
Galya. "Didn't even go in for it, I'm telling you straight."

— . . . Заче́м собрала́ вокру́г себя́ э́тих мужла́нов?
— Я не **собира́ла.** Я во́все не хоте́ла. (Бек.)
"Why did you collect these louts around you?"
"I did not collect them. I did not want them to come."

Вóльнов отвернýлся от старикá, но тот не **уходи́л**. Вóльнов спинóй почýвствовал, что Григóрий Арсéневич не ушёл и что он хóчет чтó-то спроси́ть. (Кон.)

Vol'nov turned away from the old man, but he would not leave. Vol'nov could feel behind his back that Grigorii Arsenevich had not gone away and that he wanted to ask something.

К их стóлику, прихрáмывая и подкрýчивая ус, шёл швейцáр. Тот сáмый, котóрый не **пускáл** Вóльнова в рсторáн. (Кон.)
The doorman came over to their table, limping and twisting his moustache. He was the same man who had not wanted to let Vol'nov into the restaurant.

In the following example one can feel an undercurrent of irritation at Fyodor for "not wanting to turn up":

Стёша сидéла и ждалá. Фёдор не **появля́лся**. (Тен.)
Styosha sat and waited. Fyodor did not put in an appearance.

This sense of exasperation may be extended also to inanimate objects.

Он подёргал рýчку — дверь не **поддавáлась**.
He tugged at the handle. The door would not yield.

Я не знал как зажéчь ками́н, — ýголь был кáменным; положи́л газéты, щéпки, всё бы́стро сгорéло, а прокля́тый ýголь не **зажигáлся**. (Э.)
I did not know how to light the fire. I was dealing with coal (i.e. not wood or charcoal as he would have been used to in Russia); I laid newspapers and chips of wood, everything burnt away quickly, but the cursed coal would not light.

We may note as a contrast the following example where the perfective is used without any emotive overtones.

Эрнéст Пáвлович, не поня́в ещё непопрáвимости случи́вшегося, потяну́л дверну́ю рýчку. Дверь не **поддалáсь**. (Ильф.)

Ernest Pavlovich pulled the door handle, not realising yet tha[t]
what had happened could not be put to rights. The door did no[t]
yield.

(4) Process Stressed rather than Result

This conception may be said to embrace all uses of the imper[-]
fective including those given above. Nevertheless, students o[f]
Russian often find it difficult to appreciate that the imperfectiv[e]
will be favoured in past situations where no special emphasis i[s]
laid on the result of the action and where its conclusion is n[ot]
specifically stated. Contrast the following two lines from Simonov['s]
play «Под кашта́нами Пра́ги»:

Петро́в: Вы ещё раз **прове́рили,** заме́тил он и́ли нет?
Гончаре́нко: Проверя́л сего́дня когда́ он был в ва́нно[й]
(Сим.)

Petrov: Have you checked again whether he noticed anything [or]
not?
Goncharenko: I made a check today when he was in the bat[h]
room.

Petrov is interested in whether the action of checking has bee[n]
brought to a successful conclusion; Goncharenko in the ba[re]
fact that he did carry out the action in question. Russian gramm[a-]
rians in fact call this use of the imperfective констата́ция фа́кт[а.]
We may note further examples.

Курс цини́зма я **проходи́л** не у вас, говорю́ я мра́чн[о]
(Акс.)
"It is not with you that I have been through a course of cynicism[,"]
I say morosely.

The imperfective is frequently found in this sense in questio[ns]
where the speaker knows that a certain action has been carried o[ut]

nd wishes to establish who was responsible for carrying it out.
ɔuch questions in English often have the form "Was it you who...?"

Это вы **зака́зывали** суп овощно́й?
Was it you who ordered vegetable soup?
Это вы **пуска́ли** в ход э́тот лифт?
Was it you who started this lift?

Contrast with perfective usage in:

Вы **заказа́ли** суп?   Вы **пустлий** в ход лифт?
Have you ordered the soup?   *Have you started the lift?*

In the latter cases the emphasis is now concentrated on the ques-
on of whether the action has been successfully carried out.
In cases where there is no emphasis on the completion of the
ɔtion the imperfective is more likely to be used.

Ма́рфа Петро́вна: ... Ты **подпи́сывал**, чтобы по́сле пяти́
часо́в не ходи́ли, чтобы стреля́ть? (Сим.)
Marfa Petrofna: ... Was it you who signed the order that people
were not to go about after five o'clock or they would be shot?

There is no question that the order is in force; Marfa Petrovna
 more concerned with the fact that it was treacherous for a
ussian to sign such a document.
This "neutral" form where the imperfective as it were drains
nphasis away from the verb is particularly common with verbs
ɔ say" etc.

Ники́та Серге́евич в свое́й ре́чи в Новосиби́рске **подчёркивал,**
что... (MP.)
In his speech in Novosibirsk Nikita Sergeyevich stressed that ...

In conversation он говори́л is heard more frequently than он
азал. Similarly обраща́л внима́ние frequently replaces обрати́л
има́ние in both conversational and literary usage.

(5) Expressions Normally Used with the Imperfective Aspect

A. A. Spagis* gives a list of some expressions which are normall
followed by the imperfective:

По суббо́там, обы́чно, обыкнове́нно, то и де́ло, в час
о́тдыха, в мину́ты волне́ния, час о́т часу, день ото дня, по
стоя́нно, с ка́ждым днём, по це́лым часа́м, по ме́ре чте́ни
по ме́ре продвиже́ния, це́лый день, два го́да, оди́н ме́сяц, в
ча́ще и ча́ще.

Положе́ние усложня́лось **день ото дня́.**
The position got worse from day to day.

Where such phrases are used to denote repetitive action the u
of the imperfective is obligatory.

С 1929 го́да **ре́дкий год** обходи́лся без того́, что́бы не по
вля́лся какое-нибудь но́вое произведе́ние Гри́на. (Су
дела, Москва, 1962.)
From 1929 rarely a year went by without some new work
Greene's appearing.

Ка́ждый ве́чер **проси́живали** два часа́ за уро́ками.
Every evening we sat for two hours over our lessons.

However, in a few isolated cases when some of the phrases a
expressing continuous action they may be used in conjunction wi
a perfective verb.

Весь день я **просиде́л** у себя́ в кабине́те.
I sat in my study all day.

Here the imperfective сиде́л would be equally acceptable.

Всё ча́ще и ча́ще **ста́ли** раздава́ться вы́стрелы.
Shots were heard more and more frequently (lit. began to soun

---

* А. А. Спагис, *Об употребле́нии ви́дов,* Ру́сский язы́к для студе́нт
иностра́нцев, Москва́, 1960.

In this case it would not be possible to use an imperfective verb *to begin*. Only if the idea of habitual action were intended could the imperfective be used in cases such as the following:

Это **произошло** в часы́ о́тдыха.
This happened during our free time (i.e. происходи́ло would mean *used to happen*).

Sometimes a change of aspect may introduce a new shade of meaning into the expression itself.

По ме́ре продвиже́ния они́ **уви́дели** далёкие холмы́.
As they advanced they saw distant hills.
По ме́ре продвиже́ния они́ **ната́лкивалисъ** на следы́ люде́й.
As they went along they came on traces of people.

With the expression по ме́ре чте́ния the perfective is often to be preferred.

По ме́ре чте́ния он **убеди́лся** в том, что ничего́ не знал об э́том предме́те.
As he read on he became convinced that he knew nothing about the subject.

The imperfective убежда́лся would also be possible in this case, again with an idea of "process".

B. PERFECTIVE ASPECT

(1) Verbs Expressing the Beginning of an Action

The most common prefix for indicating an inchoative verb is
за–. Students will already be familiar with such verbs as запла́-
кать, захоте́ть, закрича́ть.

> Около полу́ночи в тюре́мных коридо́рах начало́сь дви-
> же́ние, **захло́пали** две́ри, раздали́сь гро́зные о́крики. (Тол.)
> *About midnight people began to move about in the corridors of the
> prison, doors banged and threatening shouts could be heard.*

The English translation will frequently dispense with the word
"to begin".

> ... Распахну́лась дверь, и на освещённый двор вы́валились
> лю́ди, **завизжа́л** под ва́ленками снег. (Тен.)
> *... the door flew open and people poured out into the light. The
> snow squeaked under their felt boots.*

With verbs of motion the beginning of an action is normally shown
by the prefix по–:

> Он пошёл/пое́хал: *He started off;* Он побежа́л: *He began to run*

The prefix по– is found also in an inchoative sense with other
verbs expressing "emotion", e.g. Он полюби́л: *He fell in love
with (began to love).*

> Но стра́нно, и́менно тут, в Ки́еве, он впервы́е **почу́вствовал**
> как всё постепе́нно смеща́ется. (Нек.)
> *But curiously enough it was here in Kiev that he felt for the first
> time how everything was gradually changing (lit. "becoming
> displaced").*

Of course both the prefixes за– and по– can have many other
meanings besides those shown here (e.g. заходи́ть к: *to call upon*

застро́ить: *to cover with buildings;* поговори́ть: *to have a chat;* посиде́ть: *to sit for a while,* etc.).

Встре́тились две стару́шки, **посиде́ли, поговори́ли,** — вспо́мнили свою́ мо́лодость, **попла́кали** ...
Two old women met, sat for a while, had a chat, remembered their young days and had a cry ...

(2) Single Completed Action in the Past, including Semelfactives

Any narrative using the past tense will contain many examples of this usage. The semelfactive verbs are distinct only in that their meaning is restricted to a *single* action, though even this distinction is now becoming blurred (see p. 46).

In the following passage the semelfactives appear in bold type.

Удовлетворённый Оста́п, хло́пая шну́рками по ковру́, ме́дленно пошёл наза́д. Когда́ его́ масси́вная фигу́ра отдали́лась доста́точно далеко́, оте́ц Фёдор бы́стро вы́сунул го́лову за две́рь и с до́лго сде́рживаемым негодова́нием **пи́скнул:**

— Сам ты дура́к!

— Что? — **кри́кнул** Оста́п, броса́ясь обра́тно, но дверь была́ уже́ заперта́, и то́лько **щёлкнул** замо́к. (Ильф.)

Ostap was satisfied and started to walk back slowly with his shoe laces flopping along the carpet. When his massive figure had got far enough away Father Fyodor poked his head quickly round the door and squeaked with his long contained indignation:

"You're a fool yourself!"

"What?", shouted Ostap and rushed back, but the door was already closed and the lock just clicked.

(запира́ть/запере́ть: lit. *to lock*).

It will be seen that Russian simply uses a perfective aspect to express what would be a pluperfect in English. The adverb уже́ can be inserted to give extra emphasis to the fact that the action occurred on a more remote plane in the past.

Ужé по́здним-по́здним ве́чером они́ вме́сте **вы́пили** ка-зённого, па́хнущего бензи́ном спи́рта и до́лго сиде́ли пото́м на вла́жных по́сле дождя́ доска́х у забо́ра лесопи́лки. (Кон.)

Very late on in the evening they had already had a drink of the issue spirit which smelt of petrol, and after that they sat for a long time by the fence of the sawmill, on the planks which were wet from the rain.

(казённый: *issued by the government*).

Па́хнуть is of course *not* a semelfactive, but one of the *imperfective* verbs with the suffix –ну which were mentioned in the introduction.

In other cases no adverb may be necessary. The choice of the perfective aspect is sufficient by itself to show that the verb has a pluperfect sense.

Ведь и он мог знать ра́дость, боль, волне́ние, ре́вность пусть да́же пораже́ние — и в пораже́нии есть тре́пет жи́зни — а он **предпочёл** всему́ э́тому ску́дость, нищету́ поко́я (Наг.)

He might indeed have known joy, mental pain, emotion, jealousy perhaps even defeat—even in defeat there is the quivering of life—but rather than experience all this he had preferred the meanness and emptiness of quietude.

(нищета́: *poverty;* поко́й: *peace*, often *peace of mind*).

The perfective of this particular verb предпоче́сть is not used as commonly as the imperfective предпочита́ть.

In the following example the idea of "uncompleted action" has been sufficiently dominant to allow the use of the imperfective even though the verb is plainly pluperfect in meaning. Such cases must be regarded as exceptional.

То Ипполи́ту Матве́евичу каза́лось, что он никогда́ не **покида́л** Ста́ргорода, то Ста́ргород представля́лся ему́ ме́стом соверше́нно незнако́мым. (Ильф.)
At times it seemed to Ippolit Matveevich that he had never left Stargorod, at other times Stargorod seemed to him a completely unknown place.

3) Number of Completed Actions

In certain cases, though an action may be repeated in fact, the need is felt to lay stress on the fact of its *completion* at the expense of the normal practice of using the imperfective to express repetitive action. Thus when "completion" is emphasised the perfective may be used.

Он **попро́бовал** не́сколько раз откры́ть дверь.
He tried several times to open the door.

It would be equally good Russian to keep the concept of repeated action to the fore and to use the imperfective.

Он **про́бовал** не́сколько раз откры́ть дверь.

Similarly adverbial phrases of time containing the word ка́ждый will normally require an imperfective.

Ка́ждый день я **встава́л** по́здно.
Every day I got up late.

If a native speaker is faced with the necessity of using such a phrase as ка́ждый день to express a series of completed facts he feels that it is preferable not to use this combination of words baldly with a perfective, even though it is now standing as the subject of the sentence. It would be theoretically correct to say:

Ка́ждый день **прошёл** для меня́ бессле́дно.
Every day went by without any noticeable effect (lit. *trace*) *for me.*

To eliminate the awkwardness produced by this direct linking of ка́ждый день with a perfective it would be preferable *either* to rephrase the sentence:

> Ка́ждый из э́тих дней **прошёл** для меня́ бессле́дно.
> *Each of these days went by without effect.*

or to supply further context:

> Все э́ти дни я про́сто спал, и ка́ждый день **прошёл** для меня́ бессле́дно.
> *All these days I simply slept and every day went by without effect.*

Once the word ка́ждый is used apart from these set adverbial phrases there is less constraint about coupling it with perfectives.

> Стоя́ла дли́нная о́чередь. Ка́ждый покупа́тель **подошёл** к ка́ссе, **заплати́л** три рубля́ и **верну́лся** к продавцу́.
> *There was a long queue. Each customer went up to the cash desk, paid three roubles and went back to the salesman.*

The imperfectives подходи́л, запла́чивал and возвраща́лся would be equally correct in this sentence, the choice of aspect now being decided by the question of "process" or "result". Note that even semelfactive verbs may be used in such cases to express a series of repeated actions.

> Ди́зель ещё не́сколько раз, всё ти́ше и заду́мчивее, **вздохну́л** и зати́х (Кон.)
> *The diesel sighed a few more times, ever more quietly and thoughtfully and fell silent.*

(4) Extent of Time Viewed as a Completed Whole

Isachenko (*op. cit.*, p. 133) quotes two examples with different perfective forms from жить:

Он **пе́режил** ужа́сный моме́нт.
He lived through a terrible moment.
Он **про́жил** всю жизнь в дере́вне.
He lived the whole of his life in the country.

Although one sentence refers to an action which is of very brief duration and the other to an extended period of time, in both cases the perfective is the only possible aspect. The expression всю жизнь has set a fixed time limit on the action which must be regarded as "completed" rather than "in progress". This is here the crucial factor in making the choice of aspect and the length of time over which the action has extended is irrelevant. As has been noted when an action extends over an extent of time it is particularly common to find perfectives formed with the prefix про–:

Весь э́тот недли́нный диало́г Никола́й Ива́нович **провёл** в како́м-то несво́йственном ему́ энерги́чном, напо́ристом те́мпе. (Нек.)
Nikolai Ivanovich went through the whole of this short dialogue at a dynamic, pressing pace which was normally quite foreign to him.

Два ме́сяца Ольга Вячесла́вовна **просиде́ла** в тюрьме́.
Ol'ga Vyacheslavovna spent two months in prison.

Она́ роди́лась здесь, в э́том до́ме, здесь **прожила́** всю свою́ недо́лгую жизнь. (Тен.)
She had been born here in this very house and had spent the whole of her short life here.

We have already noted (on p. 26) that there is normally a clear-cut line between phrases where the accusative case without preposition is used to express "extent of time" (imperfective aspect must be used), as against those sentences where за + accusative indicates that an action was *completed* within a given "time limit" (perfective aspect).

В служе́бных дела́х, пра́вда, повезло́ — рабо́тники в обо́их сбы́тах оказа́лись операти́вными, реши́тельными, всё **ула́дилось** за день. (Вас.)

It is true that he was lucky in his official business: the staff in both the distribution points turned out to be efficient and decisive, and everything was arranged in a day.

Вот про́жил я шестьдеся́т три го́да. Мно́гое за э́то вре́мя **уви́дел**, мно́гое **сде́лал**. (Нек.)

I have now lived sixty-three years. During this time I have seen much and done much.

Гла́вное, что она́ **умудри́лась** за э́ти го́ды не растеря́ть то, что с во́зрастом обы́чно исчеза́ет — она́ оста́лась тако́й же увлека́ющейся в рабо́те, како́й была́ и в два́дцати лет. (Нек.)

The main thing was that over the course of all these years she had been clever enough to retain a quality which usually disappears as one grows older: she was just as absorbed in her work as she had been at the age of twenty.

Note that in these cases the force of the construction with за is normally strong enough to overcome the demand for the imperfective made by the concept of continuous action. Contrast however:

Ка́ждый раз, когда́ мы проходи́ли ми́мо со́гнанных в ночно́е лошаде́й, Ру́вим спра́шивал меня́ о чём ду́мают ло́шади но́чью.

Мне каза́лось, что ло́шади ни о чём не ду́мают. Они́ сли́шком **устава́ли** за де́нь. (Пау.)

Every time that we went past the corralled horses Ruvim used to ask me what the horses thought about at night.

It seemed to me that the horses did not think about anything. They had got too tired during the day.

In this case the idea of repetitive action has persisted in keeping the verb in the imperfective aspect.

We may note a further isolated exception where за + "expired period of time" is followed by an imperfective.

За всю свою жизнь я никогда, или скажем точнее, почти никогда, не **позволял** себе этого. (Нек.)
Throughout my entire life I have never—or to be more precise—almost never allowed myself to do this.

Не позволять себе expresses repetitive action; notice once more the strong tendency to use the imperfective with a negative.

(5) Perfective with Result in the Present

Such verbs often correspond to an English present; students will already be familiar with such forms as:

Я устал.
I am tired (lit. *I have got tired*).
Мы договорились.
We are agreed (e.g., on time and place of meeting; lit. *We have reached agreement*).
Ты мне здорово **надоел.**
I'm absolutely fed up with you (lit. *You have bored me*).
Я опоздал.
I am late (lit. *I have become late*).

It is useful to contrast perfectives which express a result which is still effective with imperfectives (such as those noted on pp. 32–33) where the action is confined to the past.

Imperfective	Perfective
Эта пьеса в детстве мне **нрави- лась,** а теперь нет.	— Вам понравилась пьеса?
	— Да, **понравилась.**
I liked this play as a child but I don't like it any longer).	*"Did you like the play?"*
	"Yes, I liked it (and I still do)."

Imperfective	Perfective
Я **знако́мился** как–то со всем э́тим материа́лом, но бо́льше не по́мню о нём абсолю́тно ничего́.	Мы **познако́мились** давны́м-давно́ и мы всё ещё хоро́шие друзья́.
I was once familiar with all this material, but now remember absolutely nothing about it.	*We became acquainted long ago and we are still good friends.*

Similar use is made of many verbs which express a change in the physical state of the subject. Lebedeva* divides them into two groups.

(a) Verbs expressing a change which is more or less restricted to the moment in question, e.g. вспоте́ть, побледне́ть, покрасне́ть, похолоде́ть, проголода́ться, сконфу́зиться.

As examples of this group we may quote:

Во́льнов чу́вствовал, как **затверде́ли** от хо́лода щёки и гу́бы. (Кон.) *Vol'nov felt his cheeks and lips stiff with cold.*

Я **остервене́л** и бью, бью, бью. (Акс.)

I have worked myself into a frenzy and am beating, beating, beating.

— Ишь ты, так **раскрича́лся,** — насме́шливо говори́т Ди́мка (Акс.)

"Look how excited you have got," says Dimka with a sneer.

(раскрича́ться: lit. *to work oneself into a state with shouting*).

Что же вы молчи́те? **Потеря́ли** дар ре́чи? (Сим.)

Why are you so silent? Have you lost the gift of speech?

Arising from this first group we find the very frequent use of the perfective gerund to express a gesture or a posture.

---

* Г. Ф. Лебедева, Об изучении перфектного значения глагольных форм прошедшего времени совершенного вида с китайскими учащимися, Сборник методических статей, МГУ, 1959.

Старпо́м стоя́л на мо́стике, широко́ **расста́вив** но́ги, **уткну́в-шись** гру́дью в рукоя́ти штурва́ла, и напева́л свою́ люби́-мую пе́сенку . . . (Кон.)

The first mate was standing on the bridge with his feet spread wide apart and his chest propped against the spokes of the wheel singing his favourite song (lit. *having spread his feet, having leant against*).

Офице́р ме́дленно кури́л, **навали́вшись** на ло́коть. (Тол.)

The officer was smoking at his leisure, leaning on his elbow (lit. *having leant his weight onto his elbow*).

We may note that many verbs with infinitives ending in –нуть are used in similar contexts. Thus я замёрз means *I am frozen*, я промо́к means *I have got soaked* (from infinitives замёрзнуть and промо́кнуть respectively).

(b) Verbs expressing a more permanent change, e.g. постаре́ть, похуде́ть, пополне́ть, похороше́ть, помолоде́ть, соста́риться.

Many other examples come to mind where the perfective in Russian is used to convey an idea equivalent to an English present or present perfect.

Э́то ве́рно. **Убеди́л.** (Сим.)

That is true. You have convinced me.

Ру́сские **на́чали** наступа́ть и **подошли́** бли́же. (Сим.)

The Russians have begun to advance and have come closer.

. . . озорни́к был, я зна́ю. А сейча́с **прити́х.** (Сим.)

. . . *(he) used to be quite a playboy, I know. But now he has quiet-ened down.*

(озорни́к: lit. "*a mischievous child*").

Уви́дев му́жа, Ма́рья Па́вловна сказа́ла:

–**Стрясло́сь** что-нибу́дь? (Вас.)

When she saw her husband Maria Pavlovna said: "Is something up?"

Вы, товáрищ комиссáр, комý-нибудь прикажи́те ваш пистолéт почи́стить, а то у вас в дýле **наби́лось** — не вы́стрелит. (Сим.)
Order someone to clean your pistol, sir. Otherwise you will find that the barrel is blocked and it won't fire.
(набивáться/наби́ться: lit. *to cram with something*).

Вот смотри́те. А éсли у плáнового отдéла отхвати́ть? Они́ там широкó **раски́нулись.** На шесть человéк почти́ двáдцать мéтров. Стéнки мы перенесём, отштукатýрим. (Вас.)
Now look. Supposing we take some room from the planning department? They have fairly spread themselves out in there with almost twenty square metres for six of them. We will move the walls back and re-plaster them.

Полюби́ть, the perfective of люби́ть, means literally *to fall in love with*, but is often used to signify that "one still loves".

Автобиогрáфия состои́т не из описáния самогó себя́, а из описáния всегó, что ты **уви́дел** и **полюби́л** на свéте. (Сол.)
An autobiography is not a description of oneself, but of everything that one has seen and loved on the earth.

Note the following contrast between полюби́ть and the imperfective which shows that love in this case no longer exists.

— Я **полюби́ла** человéка, и он меня́. Неужéли мы не мóжем остáться друзья́ми.
— А Ди́мка?
— Что Ди́мка? Я **люби́ла** его. Он моя́ пéрвая любóвь, а сейчáс ... другóе ... я и он ... Григóрий и я ... (Акс.)
"I have fallen in love with someone and he is in love with me. Can I not remain friends with you all the same?"
"And Dimka?"
"What about Dimka? I used to love him. He was my first love, but now things are quite different ... he and I ... Grigorii and I ..."

The next example provides a contrast between what "has survived" into the present (perfective) and unsuccessful "attempts to destroy it" (imperfective).

Афи́нский акро́поль **пе́режил** не то́лько духо́вно, но и матери́ально жили́ща разли́чных люде́й, кото́рые в тече́ние двадцати́ пяти́ веко́в его́ стара́тельно **разруша́ли.** (Э.)
The Athenian Acropolis has outlived not only spiritually but also materially the dwellings of various people who have been laboriously trying to destroy it over the course of twenty-five centuries.

The sense of action continuing into the present is found particularly with verbs of motion.

Винты́ всё быстре́е и быстре́е и слива́ются в бе́лые круги́. Стра́шный рёв. Самолёт **пое́хал.** (Акс.)
The propellers (spin) faster and faster until they become white circles. There is a frightening roar. The aeroplane has started to move.

This sense of the past perfective is often extended to form a type of first person imperative.

Ну я пошёл.
I'm on my way.
Пое́хали/пошли́.
We're off.

6) Idioms and Expressions used with the Perfective

The list given below cannot pretend to be exhaustive, but it may provide a degree of guidance in a subject which is inclined to depend purely on subjective factors.

. . . он **взял вдруг** и поцелова́л ее (Нек.)
He suddenly went and kissed her.
Взял вдруг (or simply взял) always conveys the idea of an action

which is completely unexpected.

> Он **чуть не** упа́л.
> *He almost fell.*
> Оди́н бычо́к **чуть не** забода́л меня́ во́зле по́чты . . . (Кон.)
> *One bullock almost butted me when I was near the post office . . .*
> Ю́рочка потопта́лся, зашёл **бы́ло** в пара́дное, но пото́м верну́лся . . . (Нек.)
> *Yurochka shuffled for a moment, made as though to go in by the front door, but then turned back.*

Note the restrictive force of the prefix по– in this sentence. It is in fact a good example of how even the most "neutral" of prefixes can alter the actual meaning of the verb, the imperfective топта́ться having the meaning of *to mark time*. бы́ло as used in this sentence gives the sense of an interrupted action, of hesitation, or of a desire which is quickly suppressed.

> — Что за издева́тельство! — воскли́кнул Воробья́нинов, нача́вший **бы́ло** освобожда́ться из-под и́га могу́чего интелле́кта сы́на туре́цкого-по́данного. (Ильф.)
> *" Do you think you can laugh at me?" exclaimed Vorob'yaninov, who had been on the point of trying to free himself from the yoke of the mighty intellect of the Turk's son.*
> (сы́на туре́цкого-по́данного: lit. *of the son of the Turkish subject*)

бы́ло is also frequently coupled with the past tense of хоте́ть in the sense of "would have liked to".

> Она́ **хоте́ла бы́ло** э́то сказа́ть, но не рискну́ла.
> *She would have liked to say this, but did not dare.*

> Ма́ма люби́ла гла́дить по волоса́м до тех пор, **пока́ я не** устро́ил ей сканда́л из-за э́того. (Акс.)
> *Mother used to like stroking my hair until finally I made a scene with her about this.*

A clear distinction must of course be drawn between пока́ не (*until*) with the perfective and пока́ without не (*while*) which i

normally followed by the imperfective to express an idea of continuity.

Пока́ я вам **чита́л** их (стихи́), вам бы́ло ле́гче предста́вить
себе́, что с ва́ми не я . . . (Нек.)
*While I was reading the poetry to you it was easier for you to
imagine that it was not I who was with you.*

II. Present Tense

As THE present can be only imperfective, strictly speaking it should
not be necessary to treat it in dealing with the aspects. Its usage in
Russian, however, overlaps with concepts belonging to both the
past and the future and it seems appropriate to mention these
briefly before passing to a study of the future proper.

(1) Equivalent to English Present Perfect

Like most European languages Russian uses the present as the
equivalent of the English forms "I have been doing" etc. in cases
where the action is still continuing.

> — Ско́лько вре́мени вы **живёте** в Москве́?
> — Я **живу́** здесь шесть ме́сяцев.
> *" How long have you been living in Moscow?"*
> *"I have been living here for six months."*
> Я ведь тебя́ давно́ **зна́ю,** давно́-давно́. (Оку.)
> *I have known you for a long, long time.*

(2) Historic Present

Russians allow themselves much more freedom in mingling past
and present tenses than would normally be considered possible
in English. The use of the present or future is of course normal to
express indirect speech and also sometimes after verbs *to think/
hear/see*, etc.

Старуха не плакала, рассказывала с удовольствием. — В булочную ходила, пришла, **слышу** — **ходят**, приехал хозяин, **думаю.** Тебе записка оставлена. Третьего дня приходили, оставили записку. (Пан.)

The old woman did not cry, she told her story with pleasure. "I went to the baker's, came back here and heard people walking about, so I thought the owner must have come. There is a note left for you. Someone came the day before yesterday and left a note."

For a study of these usages see D. P. Costello, "Tenses in indirect speech in Russian", *Slavonic Review*, London, June 1961. Professor Costello's conclusions might be summarised as follows: (1) After actual verbs "to speak" it is obligatory to preserve the tenses which would have been used in direct speech; (2) after the verb думать occasional exceptions to this rule are found; (3) after полагать, казаться it is possible to break the Russian norm of tense sequence and to use a past tense after a verb in the past (as is usual in English); (4) the past normally follows the verbs: видеть, быть видно.

Similar usages of course occur with the future where appropriate.

Все уверяли, что кто-то скоро **«выступит»**; одни считали, что **выступит** генерал Корнилов, другие — что **выступят** большевики. Я понял, что ничего не **пойму**, и уехал в Москву. (Э.)

Everyone kept asserting that soon someone would "show their hand"; some thought that General Kornilov would come out into the open, others that the first move would be made by the Bolsheviks. I realised that I would make no sense of anything, and went away to Moscow.

Frequently the verb to say/think, etc. is merely understood.

Торжество отлёта новой советской машины прошло без меня. Война объявлена. Я оскорбил Бабичева.

Сейча́с они́ **вы́валятся** ку́чей из воро́т аэродро́ма. Шофёры
уже́ проявля́ли де́ятельность. Вот баби́чевская си́няя маши́на.
Шофёр Альперс ви́дит меня́, де́лает мне зна́ки. Я повора́-
чиваюсь спино́й. Мои́ башмаки́ запу́тались в зелёной лапше́
травы́. (Ол.)

The ceremony of the take-off of the new Soviet plane took place
without me. War had been declared. I had insulted Babichev.

In a few minutes they would be pouring in a mass out of the aero-
drome gates. The drivers were already showing signs of activity.
Here is Babichev's blue car. The chauffeur Al'pers sees me and is
making signs to me. I turn my back on him. My shoes have be-
come entangled in the green strands (lit. *noodles*) *of the grass.*

As an extension of this idea the present is often used simply to
put a scene more vividly before our eyes.

Това́рищ Неча́ев перевяза́л команди́ра полка́, как мог, и
всё **сиди́т** во́зле него́, мо́крый плато́к ему́ **кладёт** на лоб,
про́бует узна́ть про полк, да про его си́лы, да про его зада́чу,
а тот ничего́ не **ви́дит** и не **слы́шит** . . . (Казч.)

Comrade Nechayev bandaged the regimental commander's wounds
as well as he could and sat beside him all the time, applying a wet
handkerchief to his forehead, trying to find out about the regiment,
its strength and the task allotted to it, but the commander could
neither see nor hear anything.

Купи́л биле́т, за́нял о́чередь. А передо мно́й они́ и **стоя́т** —
пять челове́к. (Ант.)

(I) bought a ticket and took my place in the queue. And there they
were, standing in front of me, five of them.

Although such examples have something of a popular flavour
the introduction of the present into narrative in the past is per-
fectly legitimate in the most purely "literary" style of prose.

. . . тепе́рь он (за́пах пре́лого се́на) держа́лся в лесно́м во́здухе
тако́й лёгкой, тако́й то́нкой пре́лестью, что **вдыха́ешь** его́
жа́дно и всё ника́к не нады́шешься. (Сол.)

. . . now the smell of ripe hay hung in the air of the woodlands in such a light and subtle fragrance that you could breathe it in greedily and never have enough of it.
(пре́лесть (fem.): lit. *charm.*)

3) Present Tense as Substitute for Future

As in English the present can be used loosely to designate actions which will occur in the future. This usage is found most commonly with the verbs *to go.* It is thus used for actions in the near future:

Куда́ вы **идёте** сего́дня ве́чером?
Where are you going this evening?

The present can also be used to describe actions which will occur in the more remote future, but which constitute part of a programme already agreed on.

Э́тим ле́том он **е́дет** в Ташке́нт.
He is going to Tashkent this summer.
Ле́том мы **е́дем** на юг, а в сентябре́ **улета́ем** в США.
In the summer we are going to the south and flying to the U.S.A. in September.

In many cases the present can be used for the future with other verbs besides the verbs of motion.

Сего́дня ве́чером мы **игра́ем** в те́ннис.
We are playing tennis this evening.
За́втра мы **встаём** в шесть часо́в.
Tomorrow we are getting up at six o'clock.
За́втра мы **еди́м** в столо́вой.
Tomorrow we are eating in the canteen.
Что ты **де́лаешь** в четве́рг?
What are you doing on Thursday?

The answer to a question thus phrased will normally be given in the future tense, either perfective or imperfective according to how the person speaking views the action.

Мы **поéдем** на кáтере по рекé, **устрóим** пикнѝк, и, éсли водá не **бýдет** слѝшком холóдная, мы **бýдем купáться.**
We will go for a boat trip on the river, we will have a picnic, and if the water is not too cold we will have a bathe.

III. Future Tense

A. IMPERFECTIVE ASPECT

1) Repetitive and Habitual Action

In all forms of the verb this is the easiest type of usage to distinguish.

А И́горь **бу́дет жить** в ма́леньком посёлке, **встава́ть** ро́вно в шесть и **отсыпа́ться** на своём кро́шечном «СТБ», когда́ идёшь в ти́хую пого́ду с тра́лом и не́чего де́лать, он **бу́дет лови́ть** ки́льку и сала́ку в четы́рнадцати ми́лях от бе́рега и ка́ждый ве́чер **бу́дет возвраща́ться** в свой до́мик, к свое́й жене́, **бу́дет дёргать** торше́р за верёвочку и **удивля́ться**: «Вот жизнь, а?» пока́ не забу́дет об океа́не. (Акс.)

And Igor will live in a little village, will get up sharp at six o'clock and get the rest of his sleep on board his tiny trawler (when one is going along in calm weather with the trawl out and there is nothing to do); he will catch sprats fourteen miles off the coast, and every evening he will come back to his little house and his wife. He will pull the cord of the standard lamp and think in amazement: "That is life for you, eh?"—until he forgets about the ocean.

СТБ: се́йнер тра́улерный большо́й; сала́ка: a type of small herring.)

The first verb in the above passage is continuous, providing an introduction to the account of how Igor is going to spend every day, and the series of imperfectives describing this routine concludes with the perfective expressing the moment in time at which the repeated actions are brought to a close.

In the future the distinction is blurred between action which will be repeated in reality and potentially repeated action.

Надевай шапку, иначе я с тобой никуда **ходи́ть** не **бу́ду** (Вас.)
Put on your fur cap, otherwise I will not go anywhere with you.

Я обяза́тельно **бу́ду** тепе́рь **запомина́ть** как мо́жно бо́льше стихо́в. (Акс.)
I will certainly try now to learn by heart as much poetry as possible

The vagueness of such examples may be contrasted with the definite sense of resolution expressed by the perfective in the following extract.

Васин: . . . Что ж, други́м пото́м ле́гче вперёд бу́дет идти́.
Сафонов: Не хочу́ я э́того от тебя́ слы́шать. Не други́е, а мы ещё вперёд **пойдём.** (Сим.)
Vasin: . . . Well, it will be easier for other people to advance after this.
Safonov: I won't have you saying such a thing. It won't be other people, but we ourselves who will begin to advance again.

Safonov, besides wishing to express a categorical idea with the perfective future, is also impelled to use it to give the sense of "to start going forward" (supplied by the normal inchoative force of the prefix по– with verbs of motion).

The conception of a rule of conduct with general application merges with that of continuous action.

Но я **бу́ду** о́чень **стара́ться,** чтобы не подвести́ тебя́. (Кон
But I will try very hard not to let you down.

Мы **бу́дем де́лать** всё от нас зави́сящее, чтобы обеспе́чить успе́х перегово́ров. (Political speech.)
We will do everything in our power to ensure the success of the talks.

2) Continuous Action

When an author is envisaging a scene in the future he will
naturally tend to use imperfectives.

Так вот я уви́жу друго́е: ко́мната где́-то, когда́-то бу́дет
я́рко освещена́ со́лнцем, **бу́дет** си́ний таз **стоя́ть** у окна́,
в тазу́ **бу́дет пляса́ть** окно́, и Ва́ля бу́дет **мы́ться** над та́зом,
сверка́я, как саза́н, **плеска́ться, перебира́ть** клавиату́ру во-
ды́ . . . (Ол.)

*And now I will imagine another scene: a room somewhere, some
time, brightly filled with sunlight. There will be a blue basin by the
window, the reflection of the window will be dancing in the water,
and Valya will be washing, bending over the basin, and sparkling
like a fish she will be splashing and fingering the iridescent ripples
of the water . . .*

(саза́н — lit. *a fish of the carp family*, клавиату́ра — lit. *keyboard*).
In other cases one can, as it were, picture a narrative in the future, with the completed acts described by perfectives and the
longer-lasting or repeated actions by imperfectives.

Я мно́го бы дал за то́, чтобы следи́ть за ва́ми, когда́ вы
бу́дете чита́ть э́тот изуми́тельный расска́з. Следи́ть за те́м,
как **бу́дут темне́ть** и **наполня́ться** слеза́ми ва́ши глаза́, как
бу́дете хму́рить бро́ви и **куса́ть** гу́бы, как вдруг **улыбнётесь**
и неслы́шный смех **задрожи́т** в ва́шем го́рле. (Пау.)

*I would give a great deal to watch you when you are reading this
wonderful story—to watch how your eyes will go dark and fill with
tears, how you will wrinkle your brows and bite your lips, how you
will suddenly smile and silent laughter will tremble in your throat.*

3) Uncompleted Action

When the speaker has to bear in mind that he may not be able
to set a definite term to his action he will tend to use an imperfective.

Вы́зовите мне карау́льного нача́льника! Бы́стро! Я бу́ду
ждать здесь. (Сим.)
Get the guard commander for me! Quickly! I will expect him here

If the perfective were to be used in this sentence it would be
less categorical and imply that there was no special urgency.

Сего́дня в во́семь они́ **бу́дут про́бовать** прорва́ться из го́рода
у Се́верной ба́лки, вдоль лима́на. (Сим.)
*At eight o'clock tonight they are going to try to break out of the
town along the estuary at the North Ravine.*

As has been noted with the past tense the most obvious example
of uncompleted action occur when one prolonged act in the imperfective is interrupted by another in the perfective.

Ты **бу́дешь** здесь **сиде́ть,** пока́ я не приду́.
You will wait here until I come.

In some cases the imperfective future gives an overtone of
unwillingness or uncertainty.

… во́лей-нево́лей **бу́дут** меня́ **учи́ть,** и я **ста́ну** те́хником
изыска́телем. (Вор.)
*… whether they want to or not they will teach me and I will be-
come a qualified prospector.*
— Това́рищ капита́н, а вон «Седьмо́й», да? А мы к нему
подходи́ть не **бу́дем?** — кри́кнул с па́лубы бо́цман. (Кон.)
*"Look, sir, that's boat number seven over there, isn't it? Are we
not going to go over to them?", shouted the boatswain from the
deck.*

Although the last example shows an imperfective with a negative
there is, in contrast to the usage in the past tenses, no general
tendency to use the imperfective with the negative in the future.
On the contrary, when the speaker wishes to deny that a given

ction will take place the perfective will be much more frequently
ound.

И по́нял, что меха́ник никогда́ бо́льше не **вста́нет**. (Кон.)
And he realised that the engineer would never get up again.

Spagis (p. 366) points out that the imperfective future is used in
any cases where up to the moment of speaking there has been
habitual action which will now be discontinued. She quotes:

Я не **бу́ду** бо́льше **заходи́ть** к нему́.
I will no longer go and visit him. (i.e. it is implied that "*I have been
to see him frequently in the past.*")

) Process Stressed rather than Result—Subjective Choice of Aspect

Often the imperfective hints at a possibility of difficulty (cf.
finitive).

Васи́лий веле́л переда́ть, что за́втра но́чью **переправля́ть**
люде́й **бу́дет**, что́бы не стреля́ли. (Сим.)
*Vasilii told me to give you a message that he will be sending some
people over to-morrow night, that we are not to shoot.*

Стря́пков злора́дно поду́мал: — В понеде́льник, тебе́, ма́туш-
ка, бу́дет не до нови́нок. Дела́ **сдава́ть бу́дешь**. (Вас.)
*Stryapkov thought gleefully: " On Monday, old girl, you will not
have time to think about new things to do. You will be handing
over your duties."*

(нови́нка — *novelty*.)

А **помира́ть бу́ду**, пе́сни петь мо́жно? (Сим.)
And if I am going to die, can I sing something then?

It is possible to make a broad classification of Russian verbs
o two categories; (1) terminative verbs where the dominant
a is that of completed action (e.g. реша́ть/реши́ть) and (2)
rative verbs used mainly to describe an action continuing over
eriod of time (e.g. сиде́ть/посиде́ть).

Both types of verbs may exist as aspectival pairs, but particularly in the future the form most commonly used will tend to be the perfective for terminative verbs and the imperfective for durative verbs. Thus one finds, for example:

Но éсли не **вы́йдет,** я тебя́ **вы́секу.** (Ол.)
But if it doesn't turn out right I will thrash you.
Зáвтра навéрно я **получý** письмó.
To-morrow I will probably get a letter.

In this case it would be impossible to substitute the imperfective (я бýду получáть) unless there was some additional idea of repetition or prolonged action.

On the other hand отмечáть/отмéтить (*to celebrate a holiday*) is a verb which is used mainly with an idea of duration; one is interested, so to speak, more in the festivities which may go on all night than in the result on the following day. Russians would seldom feel tempted to use a perfective in a case such as the following:

Как вы **бýдете отмечáть** прáздник?
How are you going to celebrate the holiday?

though they might in the past use either aspect:

Мы **отмечáли/отмéтили** прáздник на дáче.
We celebrated the holiday at our house in the country.

The vast majority of verbs in Russian, however clearly they may belong to the terminative category, have a wide range of functions in which it is possible to employ either aspect. This area of overlap is particularly large in the future where so much depends on how the speaker views the action. The choice of aspects is purely subjective. Consider the following series of perfective verbs:

Зáвтра я **напишý** óтзыв, **закóнчу** статью́, **состáвлю** экзаменацио́нные билéты . . .
To-morrow I will write a testimonial, finish my article, make examination questions . . .

Another person might use imperfectives to describe exactly he same actions. The English translation would remain unhanged.

In some cases the use of the imperfective may convey a nuance f doubt as to whether the action can be completed. This may be ompared with similar concepts expressed in the section on the nperfective infinitive (pp. 124–125—difficulty, etc.)

За́втра мы **бу́дем распределя́ть** пятику́рсников.
To-morrow we will arrange what jobs the fifth-year students are going to (after the completion of their course).

Here the perfective might readily be substituted if the speaker as more certain that it would be possible to make all the students' ppointments within the space of the following day.

Another factor leading to the wide use of imperfectives is that e speaker may have a comparatively restricted educational ackground.

Сейча́с, Татья́на Алексе́евна, я **бу́ду** вам пла́тье **гла́дить.**
По́сле того́ я **бу́ду за́втракать** а пото́м я **бу́ду мыть** посу́ду.
Now I am going to iron your dress for you, Tatyana Alekseyevna. After that I will have breakfast and then I will do the washing-up.

The maid perhaps views the day as an endless series of actions be gone through; her mistress who is more impatient to see the tions completed may correct her:

Вы хоти́те сказа́ть, Ма́ша, что вы **вы́гладите** моё пла́тье, **поза́втракаете, вы́моете** посу́ду и **отнесёте** на по́чту пять бандеро́лей — до обе́да.
You mean, Masha, that you will iron my dress, have breakfast, do the washing-up and take the five parcels to the post—before dinner.

андеро́ль: *a small parcel*)

One would have to be a mind-reader to say whether Mash
really intends to procrastinate by using the imperfective; it i
equally possible that these are simply the forms that come mos
naturally to her and that she has some uncertainty about formin
the correct perfectives (вы́гладить, поза́втракать, вы́мыть
Similarly foreigners learning Russian are often led to depen
heavily on the imperfective future as бу́ду, бу́дешь is compara
ively simple to conjugate. All things being equal, however, it
normally preferable to use the correct perfectives to describe
series of actions in the future.

(5) Questions

The imperfective future can carry more emphasis in speech and
more polite than the perfective, hence it tends to be favoured i
conversational language to give extra stress to a question. Compai
the standard phrases for asking passengers standing in the gan;
way whether they intend to alight at the next stop:

Вы бу́дете выходи́ть?

Вы бу́дете сходи́ть сейча́с?

The present is also heard (Вы выхо́дите/схо́дите на сле́дую
щей?) and occasionally the perfective future of сойти́: Вы сойдё
сейча́с?), but never the perfective of вы́йти. Though Russians adm
that this form would be impeccable from the grammatical poi
of view, they find that it cannot be pronounced with enough for
to make the question clear, perhaps because of the fact that tl
stress falls on the prefix. In questions such as these the imperfecti
is used to give a note of urgency (these examples may be contraste
with its use to lend vagueness to a statement, as seen in section (
above). Some native speakers explain the preference for the impe
fective in questions as a politer form; once more, whichev
explanation is chosen probably depends on the psychology of tl
individual and the tone of voice in which the question is pu
Further examples are given below.

Вы **бу́дете допла́чивать** пять копе́ек?

Are you going to pay the extra five kopecks? (*to make up the required amount for the purchase in question*).

Вы **бу́дете** сейча́с **ку́шать**?

Are you going to eat now?

In this case the choice of a perfective would limit the sense of the ⸗rb more than the speaker considers desirable, and hence the ⸗ore "neutral" imperfective is preferred (as against поку́шать: ⸗ *eat a little*, or ску́шать — transitive: *to eat up*).

B. PERFECTIVE ASPECT

) Single Action in Future

) Near Future

Where other considerations do not intervene the perfective will ⸗ used for a single action in the future.

Я сейча́с **узна́ю.**

I will find out straight away.

Извини́, Кузьма́ Его́рович, у нас сейча́с чи́сто семе́йный разгово́р **пойдёт.** (Вас.)

Excuse me, Kuz'ma Yegorovich, we are going to have a conversation now which must not go outside the family.

Сжима́ю ружьё так, что но́ют па́льцы. Жду, когда́ на меня́ **налети́т** у́тка. (Вор.)

I grip the shot-gun so tightly that my fingers ache. I wait for a duck to fly in my direction.

Similarly the perfective is employed for a narrative containing a ⸗ies of actions. If we have quoted the following passage at length ⸗s in order to make it clear that, notwithstanding the remarks in ⸗ first section of this chapter, the perfective future is much more ⸗mmonly found than the imperfective and should be regarded as ⸗ normal usage in most circumstances.

Вася следил за его движениями, которые он каждый вечер наблюдал всё в той же последовательности. Он удивлялся как его отец никогда не **собьётся**: не **развернёт** газет раньше, чем **выпьет** последний глоток, не «**промакнёт**» усы раньше, чем **вытрет** рот. Вася знал, что отец бегл **просмотрит** первую страницу, затем, мимо второй, чут **задержится** на третьей и внимательно **просмотрит** чет вёртую, где все заметки очень маленькие и каждая помещена в особую рамку. Потом он **свернёт** и **отложит** газету и подержав Васю на прицеле круглых очков, **спросит**:

— Ну, как наши успехи?

Вася **покажет** ему дневник, который отец **проглядит** обяза тельно с первой страницы, **упрекнёт** Васю за тройк полученную в прошлой четверти по арифметике и за отп чаток Васиного большого пальца на белой бумаге, в каку обёрнута обложка дневника.

— Готовь уроки, **скажет** отец, — а я немного **почитаю**.

Ляжет с книгой в руках на диван и тут же **уснёт**, вплоть д того часа, когда надо ложиться спать по-настоящем (Наг.)

Vasya was watching his movements which he observed him ma in the same order every evening. He wondered how his father nev made a false move; never would open the paper before drinki his last mouthful, would not dry his moustache before wiping mouth. Vasya knew that his father would run his eye quickly ou the first page, then, skipping the second, would barely pause at third, and would study the fourth page attentively, where all news items are very small and each is in its own little frame. Th he would roll up the paper, lay it on one side and training his rou spectacles on Vasya he would ask:

"Well, how is the work going?"

Vasya would show him his report book which his father would unfo ingly look through right from the first page, would reproach Vas for the "three" which he got last term in arithmetic and for

*mark left by Vasya's thumb on the white paper which had been
put round the cover of the report book.*
" *Prepare your lessons*," *his father would say*, " *while I have a bit
of a read*."
He would lie down on the sofa with a book in his hands and immediately go to sleep, right through until it was really time to go to bed.

Дневник: here, *daily record of school work*. Marks are awarded out
f five. Rough equivalents might be: пятёрка, *excellent;* четвёрка,
ood; тройка, *fair;* двойка, *unsatisfactory*. Единица is in practice
ardly ever given.)

It should further be noted that the perfective future is frequently
e equivalent of a future perfect in other languages (e.g. French)
r of an English present perfect.

Верни мне эту книгу, пожалуйста, после того как ты **посмотришь** её.
Please let me have this book back after you have looked at it.
Когда вы **кончите** это играть, доставьте мне удовольствие,
пожалуйста, сыграйте что-нибудь Вагнера. (Сим.)
*When you have finished playing this piece give me the pleasure please
of hearing something of Wagner's.*

) **Affirmation**

It does not matter in what vague future the action may be situ-
ed; the important factor is that the speaker should envisage it
being eventually completed.

Чего я не **сделаю** для вас! (Сим.)
What would I not do for you?
Рано или поздно она **позовёт** меня. И я поеду. (Кон.)
Sooner or later she will call me, and I will go.
Найдётся и для тебя, Сузи, какой-нибудь чудак. (Пау.)
Some sort of strange chap will turn up for you also, Susie.
— Я же говорил, что вы **начнёте** искать всяких объяснений.
(Ол.)

"*I told you (at the time) that you would begin to look for all sort of explanations.*"

Когда́ она́ ушла́, оди́н из офице́ров кри́кнул вслед, чт ско́ро её **приста́вят** к сте́нке. (Э.)

When she left one of the officers shouted after her that she woul soon find herself in front of a firing squad.

In the following two examples there is clearly an innuendo tha the chief point of interest is the unknown result of a definite action

«Что мне де́лать? — ду́мал я. — Е́сли он **разоблачи́т**, т сра́зу **вы́гонит**. И тогда́ . . . » Дальне́йшее я не представля́ себе́. (Вор.)

"*What am I to do?*" *I thought.* "*If he finds out he will throw n out at once. And then . . .*" *I could not imagine what would follo after that.*

— А я? — спроси́ла де́вушка. — Неуже́ли **оста́вите** у не́мце (Бек.)

"*And what about me?*" *asked the girl,* "*will you really leave n with the Germans?*"

(c) Denial

As has already been mentioned there is no tendency in the futu to use an imperfective with a negative. The more categorical quali of the perfective is favoured to indicate that a given action w definitely *not* take place.

— . . . На́ша о́чередь дви́гаться по́сле пе́рвого разря́д Ра́ньше середи́ны но́чи не **тро́немся.** (Кон.)

"*. . . It will be our turn to move after the first section. We will n set off before the middle of the night.*"

— Нет, нет, Воло́дя не **проговори́тся,** бу́дьте поко́йны!

"*No, no, Volodya won't let the cat out of the bag, don't worry*"

As in the case of affirmations the perfective is used to deny th something may happen even over a protracted period of tim

И я уже бо́льше никогда́ не **уви́жу** его́ — Бог милосе́рдно изба́вил меня́ от э́того. (Бун.)

And I will never in my life see it again—God in his mercy has spared me this.

Слу́чай забро́сил меня́ сюда́ ненадо́лго, ско́ро я уе́ду и никогда́, быть мо́жет, не **уви́жу** бо́льше ни мо́ря, ни э́тих высо́ких чёрных о́сенью изб . . . (Казв.)

Chance has left me here only for a short space of time: soon I shall go away and perhaps I shall never again set eyes on the sea, on these tall cottages, standing black in the autumn light . . .

Я к вам не **верну́сь** бо́льше. (Ол.)

I will never come back to you again.

Reference has already been made to the contrast between the simple idea of denial in such examples as against the implication where the imperfective future is used that the action had been a repeated one in the past.

— . . . Ты то́лько не бо́йся: к тебе́ я бо́льше **пристава́ть** не **бу́ду.**

"*. . . Only you need not be afraid: I won't come pestering you any more.*"

When it is not implicit that the future marks an end to a series of actions which have been "habitual" up to the moment of speaking, then the perfective future is the normal usage. This may be regarded as due to the desire of the speaker to emphasise that "this will not happen *even once.*"

Often this sense of denial is extended to proverbs.

Бли́зок ло́коть, да не **уку́сишь.**

So near and yet so far (lit. *Your elbow is near and yet you can't bite it*).

Proverbs will, of course, normally have a set form and no alternative version will be possible; but once we go beyond this into statements made by individuals we again enter the region of conjecture where the aspect used depends on the desire of the speaker to stress either the fact of completion of the action (perfective) or the general application of a principle to an indefinite number of occasions. In these cases there is no distinction in usage between "denial" and "affirmation".

В заключи́тельном сло́ве он то́лько доба́вил, что коллекти́в до́лжен состоя́ть из едини́ц, а не из нуле́й, и́бо е́сли приба́вить к нулю́ нуль, то **полу́чится** не коллекти́в, а нуль. (Э.)

At the end of his speech he only added that the collective must consist of units and not of noughts, for nought plus nought makes nought and not a united group.

Вся́кий раз, когда́ моё самолю́бие отчего́-либо **бу́дет страда́ть,** то зна́ю, что тотча́с же, по ассоциа́ции иде́й, **вспо́мнится** мне како́й-нибудь из вечеро́в, проведённых вблизи́ ва́шего пи́сьменного стола́. (Ол.)

Every time when my self-esteem is wounded in some way I know that by an association of ideas I shall immediately remember one of the evenings which I spent by your desk.

(d) Impossibility

Once the future is used to show that a given action cannot be carried out the usage is stabilised and a perfective aspect is the only form possible.

. . . Расстоя́ние же ме́жду ло́дками тако́е, что не **перепры́гнешь.** (Кон.)

. . . the distance between the boats is such that you could not jump across.

Он угре́лся в са́мых надёжных чащо́бах тайги́, куда́ не **прое́дет,** не **пройдёт** сейча́с по глубо́кому сне́гу ни ко́нный, ни пе́ший. (Нил.)

He had tucked himself away in the thickest parts of the forest where you could not pass now either on horseback or on foot.

The use of the second person singular (without pronoun—"one ould not") is particularly common in the concept of impossiility.

— На смерть глаза́ не **закро́ешь.** Она́ тебе́ их закро́ет. (Кон.)
"*You won't close your eyes on death. It will close them for you.*"
... за э́ти два́дцать лет всего́ бы́ло сто́лько, что и не **разберёшься.** (Нек.)
... *during those twenty years so much had happened that you could not make head or tail of it.*
Ну как ему́ **дока́жешь?** Это бесполе́зно ... (Вор.)
Well, how can you prove it to him? It's hopeless ...
Кто помеша́ть нам **посме́ет?** (Акс.)
Who will dare to stand in our way?

The reason why the perfective is almost invariably found in such ases is that the concept of repetition is excluded, and the speaker lways has the thought that "you will not be able to perform the ction *even once.*" (cf. Perfective Infinitive, section (2)—"Possiility.")

... нужны́ помо́щники. А где их взять? В отде́л ка́дров не **пойдёшь,** в те́хникум зая́вку не **отнесёшь.** (Вас.)
... *we need assistants. But where can you get them? You cannot go to the personnel department, or apply to the technical college.*
зая́вка: *claim, application*).

If the author here were to write: "You cannot go twenty times to e personnel department" the verb would then become imperfec-/e (indeterminate form)— не бу́дешь ходи́ть 20 раз ...). The ncept of repetition has almost always priority over all other rules.
The concepts of "denial" and "impossibility" are of course very ose in meaning as can be seen in the following example. Once ore the important factor is the stress on the categorical notion at the action will not take place even once.

Ведь, что бы с тобóй ни случи́лось, дожди́шко э́тот мéрзкий бýдет сы́пать и сы́пать и мóре не **шелохнётся,** и сóлнце н **вы́глянет,** и не **уви́дишь** ты горизóнта. (Акс.)
It is a certainty that whatever may happen to you this wretche rain will go on pouring and pouring down, and the sea will no stir, the sun will not come out and you will not see the horizon.

(2) Fixed Usages

In the case of most idioms there is a definite demand for the pe fective and they exist only in this aspect. We may note a few turn of phrase where the Russian future is the equivalent of an Englis present.

Хвáтит говори́ть глýпости . . .
That is enough nonsense . . . (though English can in this cas find a parallel usage in *That will be enough nonsense from you* cf. **Бýдет** с тебя́ with much the same meaning).
А я вам **скажý . . .** *But I'm telling you . . .*
Подýмаешь . . . *You just think . . .* (*i.e. don't be ridiculous*).
А я никáк не **вспóмню . . .** *I simply cannot remember . . .*
Я **предпочтý** бóлее старомóдное определéние: Брю́сов бы просвети́телем. (Э.)
I prefer (to use) a more old-fashioned definition: Bryusov was pioneer spirit. (lit. *an enlightener*)
— Агню́ша, чегó не **зайдёшь** никогдá?
"Agnyusha, why do you never come in to see us?"

A form which is used to express a sudden and unexpecte happening consists of the words вдруг or как вдруг followed t a perfective future.

Вот мы поднимáемся на ли́фте, а он **как вдруг стáнет.**
Here we are going up in the lift and it suddenly stops.

Кавале́ров свисти́т, дразня́ овча́рок, но всё возмо́жно: **вдруг** кака́я-нибудь **словчи́тся**, **порвёт** цепь и **перема́хнет** че́рез забо́р . . . (Ол.)

Kavalerov whistles and teases the sheepdogs, but anything may happen: suddenly one of them will contrive to break its chain and jump over the fence . . .

3) Perfective Future for Repeated Action

In these idioms expressing repeated action in either the present or the past the perfective is once more the only form used.

Всегда́ быва́ет немно́го жу́тко, когда́ но́чью ло́шадь **увя́жется** за тобо́й и не отстаёт ни на шаг. (Пау.)

It is always rather eerie at night when a horse insists on accompanying you and will not drop a single pace behind.

In some cases these futures can be translated by an equivalent idiom in English.

Волна́ поднима́ется всё вы́ше, пото́м та сторона́ её, кото́рая бли́же к бе́регу, должно́ быть, **заме́длит** движе́ние, так что вся остальна́я ма́сса воды́ **надви́нется** на неё, **нава́лится**, **нави́снет** над ней и вдруг **заворо́тится** в круто́й тяжёлый вал. (Сол.)

The wave rises up higher and higher, and then it must be that the side which is nearer the shore slows down its movement, so that all the rest of the mass of water will swirl forward on top of it, pile up, hang over it and suddenly turn into a steep, heavy breaker.

As we have seen in the section on the Present, Russian enjoys great freedom in the handling of tenses. Note the mixture of present and future in the following extract.

Впервы́е за э́ти дни в по́езде о́коло нас оказа́лся Ко́ля Никола́евич. Он бле́ден, утомлён. Смо́трит в окно́ и безостано́вочно ку́рит. Затя́нется, вы́пустит дым, и тут же опя́ть затя́гивается. (Вор.)

For the first time since we got on the train several days ago
Kolya Nikolayevich has appeared among us. He is pale and tired
He looks out of the window and smokes ceaselessly. He keep
drawing on the cigarette, blowing out the smoke and immediatel
draws on it again.

In the following example the future occurs inside a subordinat
clause which contains чтобы with the past tense.

Зато́ и раку́шек у меня́ всегда́ была́ полна́ аво́ська. Я пло́тн
накла́дывал их в жестяну́ю ба́нку и залива́л морско́й водо́й
что́бы, е́сли не **израсхо́дуешь** все сего́дня, хвати́ло и н
друго́й день. (Сол.)
On the other hand my mesh bag was always full of mussels
I packed them down tightly into a tin and covered them with sa.
water, so that there would be enough for the next day if the
were not all used up to-day.

The perfective can be employed not only to convey the idea c
repetition in the strict sense, but also that of habitual action.

Когда́ подка́чка во́здуха **зако́нчится,** давле́ние **сравня́ется**
(Сар.)
When they finish pumping the air in, the pressure will level off.
Как то́лько **вы́пьешь,** начина́ются сло́жные вопро́сы. (Кон
As soon as one starts drinking all sorts of complicated question
arise.
— А бума́ги, мо́жет, взял бы. Ма́ло ли чего́, вдруг **заде́**
жишься, дела́ каки́е . . . (Сол.)
"Perhaps you ought to take your papers with you. You nev
know what may happen, you may get held up suddenly, somethin
may crop up . . ."

As has already been noted вдруг with the perfective future e
presses an action which is not only sudden, but also unexpecte

(4) Number of Actions Grouped as One

This concept in the future is frequently found linked with a conditional clause. The conjunction éсли is generally understood.

Захочу́ — всех вас свине́й пошту́чно **куплю́** . . . (Вас.)
If I want to I can buy all you swine up one by one.
Нет, так де́ло не пойдёт! Ско́лько тогда́ на ка́ждого посети́-
теля **придётся** вре́мени тра́тить? (Вас.)
No, you won't be able to manage things like that! In that case how much time do you think you will have to spend on each visitor?

Тогда́ here is taking up a conditional clause which is under-
tood—"if you do things in this way, then . . ."

Не серди́тесь, е́сли то и де́ло **придётся** переноси́ться из
сего́дня в довое́нное вре́мя, а отту́да — опя́ть в ны́нешний
день. (Сол.)
Do not be angry if now and then we have to go back from today to pre-war days and from there again into the present.

In fact there is no imperfective future from приходи́ться. To
xpress a repetitive or habitual concept some such construction as
бу́дет ну́жно would have to be used. We may quote one more
xample with a "collection" of actions.

Ни в одно́м из э́тих городо́в я не быва́л. Тепе́рь они́ все
мои́. Я их **уви́жу.** (Вор.)
I have never been in a single one of these towns. Now they are all mine, I shall see them.

IV. Imperative Mood

THE person who is making a request or a command normally expects that the action in question will be carried through to a successful conclusion. It is customary therefore for most imperatives to be expressed in the perfective aspect.

A. IMPERFECTIVE ASPECT

The exceptional cases where the imperfective is favoured are both numerous and extremely important. Many of the concepts realised by the aspects of the indicative are reflected in usages of the imperative, and in this chapter we shall endeavour as far as possible to preserve the same order of section headings as in Chapter I (Past tenses).

(1) Repetitive and Habitual Action

(a) Repeated Action

The clearest call for the imperfective arises in cases where the imperative is used with some expression denoting repeated action on a number of separate occasions.

Звони́те мне **по воскресе́ньям** в де́вять часо́в.
Ring me up every Sunday at nine o'clock.
Де́лайте э́то упражне́ние **не́сколько раз.**
Do this exercise several times.

Note the change in meaning implied by the different aspects in the following cases.

Imperfective	Perfective
Поднима́йте ру́ки повы́ше.	Ру́ки по швам. **Подними́те** ру́ки.
Raise your arms higher	*Hands to the side* (lit. *along the*
(i.e. *throughout the exercise*).	*seams*; шов, шва, etc.).
	Raise the arms (*once*).

On the other hand the repetitive form of пры́гать/пры́гнуть (*to jump*) is expressed by a fresh perfective попры́гать, meaning *to jump for a period of time*. Thus we find:

Попры́гайте. *Jump up and down* (perf.).
Пры́гните че́рез э́ту кана́ву. *Jump across this ditch* (perf.).

Пры́гайте from the imperfective infinitive пры́гать is the form normally used when giving a simple command "Jump!" without any special indication as to where, when or how. This usage may be classified under побужде́ние к де́йствию (see section 4c) of this chapter.

Imperfective	Perfective
Дыши́те равноме́рно, не	**Вдохни́те, вы́дохните.** (MP)
заде́рживайте дыха́ние.	
Breathe evenly, do not hold your	*Breathe in, breathe out.*
breath.	

In the following example the insertion of the adverb иногда́ makes it clear that the imperative denotes repeated action.

— Что же я до́лжен де́лать? — простона́л Ипполи́т Мат-
ве́евич.
— Вы должны́ молча́ть. Иногда́, для ва́жности, **надува́йте** щёки. (Ильф.)
"*What am I to do?*" *groaned Ippolit Matveevich.*
"*You should be silent. Sometimes to look imposing you can puff your cheeks out.*"

Note how a few sentences later on in the same passage the imperfective infinitive reflects this idea of repetition.

— ... Не задýмывайтесь. Молчи́те. И не забывáйте **надувáть** щёки.

"*Don't start getting lost in your thoughts. Keep silent and don't forget to puff your cheeks out.*"

(b) General Rules of Conduct

The imperfective imperative can be used to give an instruction which has a general application (i.e. to correspond to the idea of "habitual action" in the indicative).

... и не **забывáйте,** что по дешеви́зне ингредиéнтов ведь э́то же достýпно для сáмых необеспéченных слоёв населéния. (Лео.)

... and do not forget that because of the cheapness of the ingredients this (drug) is obtainable even by the poorest sections of the community.

Contrast не забýдьте, which is used with reference to one specific occasion.

Не **забýдьте** взять с собóй зóнтик.

Don't forget to take your umbrella with you.

In fact the perfective is not restricted to cases of this sort, but can also be used for general rules under the idea of "warning" (see p. 101).

The imperfective imperative may be regarded as the normal usage for public notices.

Уходя́ **гаси́те** свет.

Put the light out when you leave.

Уважáйте труд убóрщицы.

No litter (lit. respect the work of the cleaner).

Соблюдáйте тишинý.

Keep silence.

In the latter two examples the perfective imperative is never used. In the case of погасѝте it would restrict the order to one specific occasion.

In some cases the perfective imperative can be used to give an instruction which may be said to have a general application.

Дéньги за проéзд и провóз багажá **опустѝте** в кáссу и **оторвѝте** билéт . . . (Notice on bus operating without a conductor.) *Place in the cash box money for your fare and for your luggage, and tear off a ticket.*

Russians will explain that the force of the perfective here is to give added precision to the idea of the exact spot where the money is to be paid. However, the difference between the aspects is so slight as to be negligible in this instance. The same notice can be seen with two imperfectives (опускáйте and отрывáйте), and native speakers when pressed will admit that it would be possible to use different aspects for the two verbs in this one sentence (e.g. опустѝте and отрывáйте). A further distinction between the aspects in these cases might be seen in the contrast between the categorical tone of the perfective expressing an order and the more polite imperfective which has about it something in the nature of a request.

(c) Rule of Conduct in Particular Circumstances

The speaker hopes that the action will not be undertaken once (and much less so on a number of occasions), but lays down a rule to be followed in cases where the need may arise.

О тех, кто тебя́ ослу́шается, **доклáдывай** мне. (Бек.)
Report to me anyone who disobeys you.
Ну, э́то ничегó, э́то пройдёт. Ты мне **напоминáй** в слу́чае чегó, бу́дешь? (Сим.)
Well, it's all right; it will pass over. You will remind me if anything should happen, won't you?
Шуршáние ми́ны — **зарывáйся** в зéмлю, **рой** её нóсом, рукáми, ногáми, всем тéлом, не испы́тывая при э́том стрáха,

не задумываясь. Котелок с перловым супом — **выделяй**
желудочный сок, **готовься, урчи, насыщайся, вытирай**
ложку о траву. Гибнут друзья — **рой** могилу, **сыпь** землю,
машинально **стреляй** в небо три раза. (Оку.)

Every time you hear the swish of a mortar bomb try to claw down into
the ground, bore into it with your nose, your hands, your feet,
your whole body —doing this without fear and without a second
thought. They give you a mess tin of pearl barley soup—you must
get your digestive juices working, get yourself ready, grumble at
the soup, then eat your fill, and wipe your spoon on the grass.
Your friends die—you have to dig a grave, shovel back the earth,
fire off three rounds mechanically at the sky.

(From infinitives: зарываться/зарыться, рыть/вырыть, вы-
делять/выделить, готовиться/приготовиться, урчать/заурчать,
насыщаться/насытиться, вытирать/вытереть, рыть/вырыть,
сыпать/насыпать, стрелять/выстрелить.)

Сыпь/сыпьте, though irregular, is the normal imperative from
сыпать. The perfective infinitives listed have been chosen for this
context and are not universally applicable.

An exhortation to behave in a certain way over a period of time
will also naturally entail the use of the imperfective.

Танцуйте, пока вам семнадцать! **Танцуйте,** и **прыгайте** в
сёдлах, и **ныряйте** в глубины, и **ползите** вверх с альпеншто-
ками, всё это ваше — весь мир. (Акс.)

Dance while you are seventeen years old! Dance, and jump in the
saddle, dive into the depths and climb the heights with alpenstocks.
Do not be afraid of anything—it is all yours, the whole world.

It will be noted that all the examples above contain some expression equivalent to a temporal or conditional clause defining
the circumstances in which the actions are to be carried out (о
тех кто ... в случае чего ... шуршание мины ... пока вам
семнадцать ...).

(2) Continuous Action

In the tenses of the indicative mood this concept overlaps on the one hand with that of repetitive action and on the other with the idea of "process rather than result". In the case of the imperative it is even more difficult to mark it off as a separate category of usage. The following extract is primarily repetitive, but also contains something of the sense of continuity.

... говорит начальнику штаба: «**Сиди** здесь, **командуй, разговаривай** с начальством по телефону, **докладывай** ему обстановку, а я пойду. Сам поведу полк высотку брать. (Казч.)

... he says to his chief of staff: "Sit here, give the orders, talk to Headquarters over the 'phone, make situation reports to them, and I will go on. I am going to lead the regiment myself to take the heights."

In certain contexts a different nuance is introduced into the meaning of the verb by the use of the imperfective aspect. Thus, for example, with оставаться/остаться the perfective will be the normal form when there is no additional overtone. A limitation in time or extent will also make it preferable to use the perfective.

Останьтесь с нами до вечера.
Stay with us till the evening.

The imperfective form has often something of a note of resignation.

Ну, что же, **оставайтесь** с нами. (Сим.)
All right then, stay with us.
А ладно, **оставайся.** Только вот что. Не читай ты больше энциклопедию. Достань книжку попроще. (Хме.)
All right. Stay on. Only look—don't read the encyclopaedia any more. Get something simpler.

In other contexts it may have the sense of "remain for ever".

Оставайтесь мне всегда верной.
Remain faithful to me for ever.

Compare also the choice of the imperfective in the following dialogue.

— Товарищ, тут входа нет.
— А я встречаюсь здесь с товарищем.
— Ладно, **встречайтесь.**
"*There is no way in here.*"
"*But I am meeting a friend here.*"
"*All right then, meet him.*"

(3) Uncompleted Action (Negative imperatives)

When the speaker does not wish to see the action being undertaken, and therefore certainly not completed, it is only natural that he should use the imperfective aspect of the imperative.

Не **напрягайтесь.**
Don't tighten up (your muscles).
«Не **падайте** духом, Боулдер и Ко. спешит к вам на помощь!» (Лео.)
"*Don't lose heart, Boulder and Co. are hastening to help you.*"
— А ты не **лезь** не в своё дело! (Вас.)
"*And don't you poke your nose into what is none of your business.*"
— Киреев, проси гостью. Не **заставляй** девушку ждать. (Бек.)
"*Kireyev, ask our guest in. Don't keep the girl waiting.*"
Не **притворяйтесь,** что вы меня не понимаете. (Сим.)
Don't pretend that you do not understand me.
И не **перебивайте,** слушайте. (Нек.)
And don't interrupt, listen.

Отверни́тесь к две́ри и, пока́ не сосчита́ю до трёх, не **пово-ра́чивайтесь.** (Роз.)

Turn away to face the door and don't turn round again until I count three.

Nevertheless if the speaker wishes to warn the other party against an accident of some sort he will use a perfective imperative. The unexpected aspect brings the force of the warning out with peculiar vividness. We find this usage frequently with some such preparatory word as смотри́.

Помоги́. Смотри́, будь осторо́жней, не **испо́рти!** (Роз.)

Help me. Look out, be careful, don't spoil it (i.e. the piece of furniture she is carrying).

(4) Process Stressed rather than Result

(a) Verbs with No True Aspectival Pair

As has been noted in the introduction, several common verbs correspond to perfectives which must be followed by a direct object, either expressed or implied. It is natural in these cases to find the imperfective as the normal form of the imperative and the perfective used only in a restricted number of instances. The imperfective has here three separate meanings: (1) Encouragement to proceed with an action which has already been specified (as examined in the next section); (2) the intransitive sense of "Carry out the action of reading"; and (3) the transitive ("Read this story", etc.). The perfective corresponds only to this latter meaning.

Imperfective	Perfective
Чита́йте!	**Прочита́йте** э́тот текст на за́в-тра.
Read! (i.e. either "*Continue reading*", or "*Start the process of reading*").	*Read* (i.e. *finish*) *this text for to-morrow.*

Imperfective	Perfective
Игра́й в па́рке ско́лько уго́дно.	**Сыгра́й** э́ту сона́ту для нас.
Play in the park as long as you like.	*Play this sonata for us.*
Пой!	**Спой** пе́сенку, кото́рую ты учи́ла в шко́ле вчера́.
Sing!	*Sing the song you learnt in schoo yesterday.*
Ку́шайте пожа́луйста.	**Поку́шайте** до отъе́зда.
Please do eat.	*Have something to eat before you leave.*

The use of the imperfective with an object is equally widespread
The narrower range of usage in the perfective is merely one more
instance of the general truth that the imperfective, as the more
neutral form, can embrace the meanings of several perfectives. A
transitive imperfective can frequently be substituted for a per
fective when it is not desired to lay special emphasis on the idea o
completion.

«Войдёт Сизо́в, а вы в бума́ги углуби́тесь. Возмо́жно он
вам наизу́сть изве́стны, но э́то нева́жно, **чита́йте** их не спеша́.
(Вас.)
"*Whenever Sizov comes in, you bury yourself in your papers
Maybe you do know them by heart, but that doesn't matter, rea
them and take your time over it.*"

The first imperative углуби́тесь introduces clearly the idea o
"immerse yourself in the process of reading (to show that yo
cannot attend to Sizov immediately)."

The verbs "to eat" use the imperfective imperative much mor
frequently than the perfective.

«Всё ты со свои́ми миллио́нами! **Жри** их тепе́рь, свой бума́ж
ки.» (Вас.)

"*You are always talking about your millions! Eat them now, your banknotes.*"

(жрать/сожрáть — pop.: *to gorge, guzzle*)

Ешь ананáсы, ря́бчиков **жуй.**
День твой послéдний прихóдит, буржу́й. (Мая.)

Eat your pineapples, munch your grouse. Bourgeois, your last day is coming. (жуй regularly formed from жевáть, cf. попрóбуй from попрóбовать etc.)

Note the change of aspects in the following extract, when the imperative is given a more definite application by the inclusion of an object.

«Тепéрь слу́шай. **Посылáй** пря́мо на квартúру к адресáту. Дай Симу́хову лóшадь . . . Нет, постóй, Симу́хова не посылáй, он, как вы́пьет, вся́кую осторóжность теря́ет. **Пошлú** с ку́чером стару́ху . . .» (Вас.)
" *Now, listen. Send it straight to the flat to the person it is addressed to. Give Simukhov a horse . . . No, wait, don't send Simukhov, he throws caution to the winds as soon as he has had a drink. Send the old woman with the driver . . .*"

In other cases verbs which are often regarded as pairs have in fact a different range of meanings. Many verbs meaning "to speak", etc. are more frequently used in the imperfective aspect in view of such considerations.

Imperfective	Perfective
Говорúте!	**Скажúте,** пожáлуйста . . .
Speak!	*Tell me, please . . .*
	. . . когдá молчáние становúлось слúшком длúтельным, Рúта обращáлась со своéй обы́чной прóсьбой:

Imperfective	Perfective
	— **Скажи** мне что́-нибудь. (Ант.) *When the silence became too prolonged Rita would turn to him with her usual request: "Say something to me."*
Дава́й, **расска́зывай.** *Come on and tell what happened.*	**Расскажи́те** анекдо́т. *Tell me a joke.*
Дава́й, Стря́пков, **докла́дывай.** (Вас.) *All right, Stryapkov, make your report.*	
«Я — Варва́ра Степа́новна. **Выкла́оывай** де́ло.» (Тен.) *"I am Varvara Stepanova. Explain what is happening."*	
Молчи́те, я вам говорю́. *Be quiet, I tell you.*	**Замолчи́те** is used to stop someone talking who has already started; молчи́те may also be used in this case (i.e. the prefix за– here has its inchoative force of *begin to be silent*).

Compare also the entirely separate verb помолча́ть meaning *to be silent for a while*, e.g. one may say to someone who is monopolising an argument:

Помолчи́те мину́тку и да́йте говори́ть Алексе́ю.
Be quiet for a moment and let Aleksei speak.

As usual the imperfective forms (смотри́ and слу́шай) embrace much wider range of usage than the perfectives which restrict th application to a definite moment in time. Similarly with the ver переходи́ть/перейти́, the imperfective can be used instead of th perfective in the normal concrete sense of crossing the road, etc.

besides which it has the abstract meaning of changing from one action to another.

Переходи́те доро́гу то́лько в поло́женных места́х.
Cross the road only at the proper places.
Бего́м марш! . . . **Переходи́те** на ходьбу́.
Double march! . . . Change to quick march.
Переходи́те, това́рищи, к водны́м процеду́рам. Всего́ хоро́шего! (МР.)
Now proceed to washing operations. All the best.

Other abstract meanings are also found where no movement in the real sense is implied.

Переходи́те в другу́ю кома́нду.
Join the other team.

In contrast перейди́те is only employed when one wishes the physical action to be carried out on a specific occasion.

Перейди́те (че́рез) у́лицу здесь.
Cross the street here.

Again the perfective пойди́те will restrict the action to a definite set of circumstances.

Пойди́те к моему́ това́рищу и возьми́те у него́ э́ту кни́гу.
Go to my friend and get this book from him.

The imperfective иди́те could be substituted in such a sentence and in addition has a number of other uses where it would be wrong to employ пойди́те.

Иди́те сюда́.
Come here.
«**Иди́**, голу́бчик, вон туда́, напро́тив в шесто́й подъе́зд и подыми́сь на тре́тий эта́ж.» (Казч.)
"Go across the road there, my dear, to the sixth entrance and go up to the third floor."

The perfective aspect is often used to denote a limited period of time and where it is not desired to introduce this nuance the imperfective will be preferred.

Imperfective	Perfective
Спи!	**Поспи́** немно́жко.
Sleep!	*Sleep a little*, or *have a sleep.*
Продолжа́йте под му́зыку.	**Продо́лжите** ещё немно́го.
Continue in time to the music.	*Go on a little more.* (Note the irregular stress on this imperative.)
Продолжа́йте ходьбу́.	
Go on walking.	
«Да ты, ока́зывается, за́втракал. Сади́сь, **продолжа́й,** не сетсня́йся.» (Казч.)	
"Apparently you were having breakfast. Sit down, carry on and don't be embarrassed."	
Слу́шайте — я приду́ на вокза́л в семь.	**Послу́шайте** то, что я вам скажу́.
Listen, I will come to the station at seven.	*Listen to what I am telling you.*
Сиди́те, сиди́те, пожа́луйста.	**Посиди́те** немно́го, отдохни́те.
Please don't get up.	*Sit for a little and rest.*

With отдыха́ть/отдохну́ть the same distinction occurs between the perfective expressing "have a rest (for a while)" and the imperfective which poses no time limit. The difference is not always strongly felt and two individuals may use different aspects in identical circumstances.

Неде́лю что́бы я тебя́ не ви́дел. **Отдыха́й.** (Сим.)
I do not want to see you for a week. You are to rest.

In the examples which follow the idea of process is clearly more important than that of result.

Сами жу́льничали, са́ми и **расхлёбывайте.** (Вас.)
It was you who did the swindling, you can take what is coming to you.

... как то́лько послы́шится шум мото́ра, так бегу́т сообща́ть Мари́и: **встреча́й!** твой лети́т! (Сол.)
... as soon as the engine can be heard they run to tell Maria " Go and meet him, it is your man flying in!"

Here the infinitive is also imperfective with the same idea of emphasising the "process".

) Politeness

The imperfective imperative is used to express a request rather than an order. To express English forms such as "Won't you take a seat?" the equivalent is almost invariably сади́тесь. The perfective can be extremely curt and categorical.

— Да **ся́дьте** вы, идио́т прокля́тый, навяза́лся на мою́ го́лову! — зашипе́л Оста́п. — **Ся́дьте,** я вам говорю́! (Ильф.)
"Sit down, you damned idiot, I wish I hadn't got you round my neck!" Ostap hissed. "Sit down, I'm telling you."

(навя́зываться/навяза́ться: lit. *to foist oneself upon*.)
Да in this sentence is purely emphatic, cf. Да нет ...: *Why, no ...*
Used in a case like this ся́дьте is brusque and often downright rude. It may also be used to give a command without any of these overtones, e.g. for physical exercises:

Тепе́рь **ся́дьте** по-удо́бнее и глубоко́ подыши́те.
Now sit more comfortably and breathe deeply.

Everything in fact is dependent on the tone of voice and the context in which ся́дьте is used. Mazon (p. 91) quotes its use by a doctor to a patient:

Ся́дьте на край сту́ла.

Sit on the edge of the chair.

Similarly a waiter in a restaurant can say to a customer to lay greater emphasis on the choice of seat:

Ся́дьте вон туда́, вам бу́дет бо́лее удо́бно.

Sit over there, you will be more comfortable.

However, unless the direct tone of ся́дьте is softened by som words of this sort, сади́тесь is practically always preferred. Simi larly станови́тесь and ложи́тесь are used rather than ста́ньт (стать) and ля́гте (лечь).

There is also a widespread tendency to use the imperfectiv imperative of verbs of motion, when it is desired to express a invitation rather than a command.

Приходи́те к нам на обе́д часа́ в два.

Come and have dinner with us about two o'clock.

Заходи́ ко мне в сре́ду.

Drop in to see me sometime on Wednesday.

A nuance of politeness is intended by the use of the imperfectiv in the above examples. It is possible also to say **Зайди́** ко мн сего́дня ве́чером. However, in practice the perfective is not ofte heard, as заходи́ть sounds less peremptory. The imperative пр ди́те is only heard as an order, generally to someone in a subord nate position. In normal conversational usage it is replaced b иди́те сюда́ (*Come here*, etc.). In order to avoid any note of cur ness it is possible to say заходи́те, *Come in*, even when addressir a guest who is actually standing at the door. In the case of входи́т войди́те to answer a knock at the door, the two aspects are foun Those speakers who favour войди́те will defend their use of tl perfective by saying that входи́те carries with it an idea of побу́ж де́ние к де́йствию and is therefore less polite.

Though the perfective imperative of "going" verbs is not n cessarily impolite, the context is really the deciding factor. There is r doubt about the brusque tone of commands such as the followin

— А ты, мать, не вме́шивайся. Де́вушка, **вы́йди** отту́да. (Вас.)

"And don't you interfere, Mother. Come out of there, my girl!"

The use of де́вушка is not by itself impolite; it is in fact a normal form of address in the Soviet Union.

Проходи́ть/пройти́ in most forms exist as a pure aspectival pair. In the imperative, on the other hand, there is a clear differentiation in meaning between the two aspects.

Ма́льчик неуве́ренно сказа́л: — **Пройди́те,** пожа́луйста. (Казч.)

The boy said uncertainly: "Go on through, please." (i.e. "I will let you go through—we are willing to receive you.")

Проходи́те is more polite and is used in the sense of "The way is clear—there is no need for you to wait here." It is also used by policemen etc. in the sense of "Move along there!"

c) Encouragement

When it is clearly understood what action is going to be undertaken the imperfective is used to instigate the start of the action. As the queue files up to the cash desk in the canteen the cashier says to each new customer: зака́зывайте, i.e. *get on with the business of ordering your lunch vouchers.* Borras and Christian very aptly point out that such cases find a parallel in English in slang expressions of the type "Get going", etc. It is not suggested that this form of words should always be retained in translating these imperatives, which are not necessarily impolite. The degree of urgency and curtness they convey will be conditioned in each instance by the speaker's tone of voice and the context in which they are used.

Принима́йся за рабо́ту.

Set about your work.

. . . когда́ Черепа́нов стал ему́ пере́чить, он сде́лал вид, что рассерди́лся и сказа́л: «**Выполня́йте** приказа́ние.» (Казч.)

. . . when Cherepanov began to argue with him he pretended to ge
angry and said: " Carry out the order."

Розенберг: . . . Ка́жется, придётся вас пове́сить.
Ма́рфа Петро́вна: Ве́шай. (Сим.)

Rosenberg: . . . It seems as though we shall have to hang you.
Marfa Petrovna: Go on then and hang me.

It may seem odd to classify such an example under the heading
of побужде́ние к де́йствию, as the Russian woman really intend
to express indifference to her fate. The perfective imperative would
be used if one were giving an order:

Отведи́те его́ во двор и **пове́сьте** его́.
Take him into the yard and hang him.

In the example quoted from Simonov the action in question ha
already been defined by the German officer saying «пове́сить»
In many cases a perfective imperative will be used to specify wha
action is to be performed and will be followed up by an imper
fective to induce the person addressed to make a start on th
action.

Скажи́ мне, заче́м ты э́то сде́лал. Ну что же, **говори́.**
Tell me why you did this. Come on then, speak.

This switch of aspects occurs when reluctance or hesitation i
shown, and it may be regarded as the normal practice in Russia
that an order will be given in the imperfective in cases where ha
to be repeated.

Закро́йте дверь, пожа́луйста . . . **Закрыва́йте** же дверь, ра́д
бо́га. Стра́шно ду́ет.
*Close the door, please. Close the door, for Heaven's sake. There's
frightful draught.*

Спроси́те доро́гу у э́того милиционе́ра . . . Ну, что ж
спра́шивайте. Не стесня́йтесь.
*Ask that policeman the way . . . Go on then and ask him. Don't l
embarrassed.*

) Fixed Usages

Several verbs have already been noted (pp. 87–92 above) where the
fference in meaning between two aspects conventionally regarded
a pair is sufficient to enforce the use of one or other in specific
•ntexts. In other parts of the verb the addition of a prefix may
ive no effect beyond that of forming a "true" perfective. Thus
• смотре́л means *he looked*, whereas он посмотре́л simply means
took a look; in this case the prefix does not introduce any extra
iance beyond that of completing a single action which is the
•rmal function of the perfective. In the imperative forms, how-
•r, the two aspects of many pairs have acquired distinctly separate
•anings, so that they cannot always be interchanged.

iperfective	Perfective
лотри́, не упади́, будь осто- жен.	**Посмотри́,** не спит ли он.
atch out that you don't fall, be *•eful.*	*Have a look and see if he is* *asleep.*
•три́ (and below слу́шай) ve become, as it were, partic- in this usage and perfectives ıld not be substituted. Смо- í of course retains its normal ·ral meaning elsewhere.	**Посмотри́** на меня́ мину́точку. *Look at me for a moment.*
•отри́ на меня́ и отвеча́й на й вопро́с.	**Посмотри́те,** как я вы́гляжу.
•k at me and answer my ques- *•1.*	*How do I look?*
•s interesting to note that, as a quentative form of смотре́ть •ts, a distinction can be made these imperatives between •tinuous action (смотри́те)	

Imperfective   Perfective

and repeated action as in the following example.

А са́ми вы́йдите и **посма́три-
вайте** че́рез э́ту дверь. (Сим.)
*But you go out and look through
that door from time to time.*

Слу́шай, ты не мо́жешь мне   **Послу́шай** то, что я тебе́ ‖
помо́чь ве́чером?   ворю́ . . .
Listen, couldn't you help me this   *Listen to what I am going to ↓*
evening?   *you.*

Слу́шайте радиопрогра́мму на
сего́дня, 17 ма́рта . . . (МР.)
*Here are the (radio) programmes
or to-day, 17th March . . .*

Дава́йте, when used to introduce a first person plural impera‖
is only used in the imperfective (cf. смотри́ and слу́шай).

Дава́йте, мы пойдём . . .
Let us go . . .

There is also a distinct difference in meaning between the
perfective соглаша́йся (*agree to my request*) and the perfec‖
согласи́сь (*you must admit*). Compare the following two examp‖

Ва́син: Мне на́до поду́мать.
Козло́вский: Соглаша́йтесь. (Сим.)
Vasin: I must think.
Kozlovskii: I hope you will agree.
Согласи́тесь, что на у́лице сего́дня о́чень хо́лодно.
You must agree that it is very cold outside to-day.

In the case of встава́ть/встать the perfective is restricted ‖
purely concrete meaning of *get to your feet.* The imperfec‖

mbraces both this meaning and also the more abstract senses of
ne verb where an emotive sense is introduced, e.g. the opening of
ne Internationale:

Встава́й, поднима́йся, рабо́чий наро́д . . .
Arise, working people . . .

B. PERFECTIVE ASPECT

) Normal Usage. Single Action to be Completed

Хло́пните в ладо́ши под коле́ном. **Вдохни́те** на ме́сте. Но́ги
поста́вьте поши́ре плеч.
Косни́тесь пра́вой руко́й ле́вого носка́. Пони́же **наклони́тесь.**
Наклони́ться, вы́прямиться.
Верни́тесь к исхо́дному положе́нию. **Соедини́те** но́ги. **Вдох-
ни́те.** Бего́м марш. **Оботри́те** те́ло вла́жным полоте́нцем.
(MP.)

Clap the hands under the knee, breathe in on the spot.
Stand with your feet wide apart (lit. *wider than your shoulders*).
*Touch the left foot with the right hand. Bend lower. Bend, straighten
up.*
*Back to the normal position. Legs together. Breathe in. Double
march. Wipe the body down with a damp towel.*

(Note the irregular stress on хло́пните.)

— Тепе́рь слу́шай. Снача́ла **обложи́** ва́той. По́нял? Ва́той.
Пото́м **дай** слой бума́ги. **Возьми́** в кра́сном уголке́ подши́вку
«Трудово́го кра́я». По́нял? **Перетяни́** шпага́том. То́лько
попро́буй — кре́пко ли? Бума́жный не пойдёт. **Пусти́** нату-
ра́льный. Пото́м соло́мой . . . По́нял? (Вас.)

*Now listen. First of all wrap it round with cotton wool. Do you get
that? With cotton wool. Next a layer of paper. Get some bound
copies of the "Local Worker" from the party cultural centre.*

Do you understand? Tie it up with string. But just make sure tho
it is good and strong. It's no use using paper string. Use rea
string. Then pack it in straw . . . do you understand?

А ты, голу́бчик, **разыщи́,** пожа́луйста, э́того . . . как его́ . .
Рябцо́ва и **попроси́** вы́ступить. **Скажи́,** что я ли́чно ег
прошу́ . . . (Вас.)

But you, my good chap, go and look out this . . . what's his name . .
Ryabtsov and ask him to speak. Tell him that I'm asking him as
personal favour . . .

Пове́рьте мне, в любви́ всегда́ есть како́й-то смысл. (Сим
Believe me, there is always some sense in love.

In this last case the perfective is less categorical than the in
perfective (compare войди́те and входи́те).

(2) Number of Actions Grouped as One

Sometimes the idea of the act being completed outweighs th
of repetitive action. This is especially clear in the following examp
where the expression де́сять раз enforces the use of the perfectiv
Note also the use of the imperfective imperative of стоя́ть; t
perfective посто́й has the meaning of *wait a minute.*

. . . для себя́ его́ (Ста́лина) слова́ слы́шал: «Стой, Сафоно
и ни ша́гу наза́д! **Умри́,** а стой! Дери́сь, а стой! Де́сять р
прими́, а стой!» (Сим.)

. . . I have heard Stalin's words for myself: " Stand firm, Safon
and not a step back! Die, but stand firm! Stand and fight! Let t
enemy attack ten times (lit. "receive"), but stand firm.

Дра́ться, being a verb which expresses primarily a continuo
action (compare чита́ть, стоя́ть) could not here be placed in t
perfective. Note however:

— Ма́му жа́лко, Ви́тя, — сказа́л он ба́сом. — Ты уж **пост**
ра́йся всё э́то . . . сгла́дить ка́к-то. (Акс.)

"*I am sorry for Mother, Vitya,*" *he said in a gruff voice.*" *Do try and . . . smooth this all over somehow or other.*"

Стара́ться in contrast to verbs which express primarily "conti-uous" concepts falls naturally into the perfective in such a sentence ı the sense of "make an effort". The prefix по– in this verb merely ıakes the action perfective and restricts it to the particular case ıat the speaker has in mind; and has no overtone of "try a ttle". This can be clearly seen in the usage of the future where я эстара́юсь conveys more of the idea of determination to secure a efinite result than я бу́ду стара́ться (ка́к-нибудь и когда́-нибудь).

3) Warning

The perfective is used (see p. 87) to caution against some inadver-nt action, this being contrary to the normal usage of the imper-ctive imperative with the negative and also to the imperfective ea of laying down a general rule of conduct.

Ну, до свида́ния, смотри́ не **подведи́** меня́.
Well, good-bye, and see that you don't let me down.
Pul'kina (p. 213) quotes examples:
Не **хло́пни** случа́йно две́рью.
Don't let the door bang accidentally.
(хло́пать/хло́пнуть + instrumental: *to slam*)
Смотри́, не **забу́дь** но́мер моего́ телефо́на.
Mind you don't forget my telephone number.

Pul'kina points out that in such cases both aspects are possible, ough the perfective tends to predominate. It is also quite normal say:

Пожа́луйста, не **хло́пай** две́рью.
Please, don't bang the door.

* И. М. Пулькина, Краткий справочник по русской грамматике, Учпед-, 1961.

Смотри́ не **забыва́й** нас.
See that you don't forget us.

Не забу́дьте in normal conversational usage is heard much mor
frequently than не забыва́йте, which has a solemn overtone o
"remember as long as you live . . ."

(4) Fixed Usages

The imperative is used in a number of idioms in Russian t
express conditional and optative concepts. Mazon treats idioms c
this type (pp. 68–74 and 92–94). He points out that in som
forms of popular sayings there are alternative usages according t
whether the speaker thinks of the expression as being a rule wit
general application (see p. 82) or a number of separate action
(see p. 100). Mazon lists fluctuations in usage for the following e
pressions:

Imperfective	Perfective
Ночь была́ темна́, хоть глаз **коли́.**	**вы́коли** *The night was so dark that o felt blind* (lit. *You could put o your eyes.*).
. . . тако́й во́здух, что хоть то- по́р **ве́шай.**	**пове́сь** *The air was so thick that y could hang an axe up in it.*

The imperative is freely used in other conditional sentences.
Сохрани́ Христофо́ров свою́ тре́звость и рассуди́тельност
он бы узна́л . . . (Вас.)
*If Khristoforov had preserved his sober powers of reasoning
would have found out . . .*

Омы́тый ли́внем во́здух был чист, прозра́чен.
От ло́дочной ста́нции до элева́тора до́брых три киломе́тра
в э́то у́тро каза́лось — **протяни́** ру́ку, и вот он, ря́дом, мо́ж
да́же погла́дить вла́жную бето́нную грома́дину. (Вас.)

The air was washed clean and transparent after the downpour.
It was a good three kilometres from the boat station to the elevator,
but on that morning it seemed as though you could stretch out your
hand and it would be beside you, so close that you could even stroke
its wet concrete mass.

... афи́шек пестре́вших всю́ду, куда́ ни **покоси́сь** прохо́жий.
(Тол.)
... there were gaudy notices everywhere a passer-by might look.

Тепе́рь он пи́шет то́лько теорети́ческие и крити́ческие статьи́,
избра́в свое́й специа́льностью нау́чно-фантасти́ческую и
приключе́нческую литерату́ру, — бла́го её в магази́нах хоть
отбавля́й. (Вас.)
*Now he writes only theoretical and critical articles, making his
special field science fiction and adventure literature—it's a good
thing the way the shops are absolutely crammed with the stuff
(lit. "so much that you could take it away").*

— Зна́чит, мы к вам. Так и так, что хоти́те **де́лайте,** куда́
хоти́те **дева́йте,** обра́тно в Москву́ не пое́дем. (Сол.)
*"So, we have come to you. Say what you like, do what you will,
find a corner for us wherever you like (lit. push us in), we are not
going back to Moscow."*

Something of the origins of the expressions containing хоть
(which was once the imperative of хоти́те) can be seen in examples
such as this. It would of course be impossible to substitute perfective imperatives here because of the deliberate vagueness conveyed by the expression что хоти́те.

With a fixed number of verbs of motion Russian couples imperatives giving a rough equivalent of the English "look and see", etc.

Пойди́ **купи́** сигаре́ты.
Go and buy some cigarettes.

Беги́ **узна́й,** что с ним там.
Run down and find out what is wrong with him there.

— ... А то иди **попробуй,** ищи ветра в поле. Без меня н
найдут!

" *Otherwise they can go and try—it would be like looking for t*
wind in the field. They won't find it without me!"

Note that there is no punctuation between the two imperative
In set phrases of this type the first imperative may be in either aspe
according to the context. The second imperative can of cour
only be perfective.

V. Infinitive

A. IMPERFECTIVE ASPECT

In many cases the infinitive will reflect the aspects which would have been used if the sentence had been in the indicative.

Как то́лько начнётся кипе́ние, пла́мя сле́дует **уба́вить** и **подде́рживать** сла́бый ого́нь.
(Instructions for gas stove.)
As soon as the water begins to boil the gas should be turned down and a lower heat maintained.

If the second half of this sentence were for example in the past tense, it would read: *She turned down* (уба́вила — perfective) *the gas and kept it on a lower heat* (подде́рживала — imperfective expressing continuous action).

Я ведь пригожу́сь для жи́зни. Помоги́те мне. Ведь э́то да́же смешно́ **убива́ть** челове́ка, кото́рый ничего́ не успе́л **соверши́ть.** Я да́же деся́того кла́сса не ко́нчил. (Оку.)
Look, I will be fit for life. Help me. It is even ridiculous, you know, to kill a man who has not had time to bring anything to completion. I have not even finished my tenth year at school.

In this example the imperfective infinitive убива́ть stresses the idea of a principle with general application, whereas the idea of completion is expressed in the perfective соверши́ть. The fact that the action was not in fact completed hinges on the negative coupled with the verb успе́л and in this case has no effect on the aspect used the infinitive. The question of the influence of negative + auxi-

liary on the infinitive will occupy a large part of this chapter
but first let us dispose of the simpler cases where the infinitiv
is following a similar pattern to that which we have indicate
in the other moods of the verbs.

(1) Repetitive Action

(a) Repeated Action Proper

Я до́лжен был раз в неде́лю **явля́ться** в уча́сток. (Э.)
I had to report once a week to the police station.

(Though уча́сток may still be used in the sense of "police station"
its normal current use is as a "plot of land". The accepted trans
lation for "police station" would now be отделе́ние or simpl
мили́ция).

«Ох, знать бы, ка́ждый бы день ей на́до бы́ло **писа́ть** о себ
хоть два слове́чка.» (Тол.)
*"Oh, if only I knew how she was—she ought to write every da
even if it's only two words."*

... впереди́ бы́ло ещё сто́лько высо́ток, что е́жели за ка́жду
расстре́ливать команди́ров полка́ и́ли **дава́ть** им Геро́
Сове́тского Сою́за, то не хва́тит офице́ров в а́рмии и зо́лот
в це́лом госуда́рстве. (Казч.)
*There were still so many hills in front of us that if for each one с
them you were to shoot the regimental commander or give him th
order of Hero of the Soviet Union then you would not have enoug
officers in the army nor gold in the entire country.*

Мы стара́емся **ука́зывать** на э́ту специ́фику везде́, где ок
зывается необходи́мым.
*We try to point out this feature on each occasion when it seen
essential.*

In the examples above the idea of repeated action is quite explic
and it would be impossible to use anything but an imperfectiv

nfinitive. In the example which follows, substitution of the per-
ective столкну́ться would drastically alter the meaning of the
sentence. Ино́й раз would then come to mean not *sometimes*, but
on another occasion.

То, с чем приходи́лось ино́й раз **ста́лкиваться** в общежи́тии . . .
(Пан.)
What he had sometimes had to meet with in the hostel . . .

In the next example a perfective infinitive is used in spite of the
fact that action on a number of occasions is clearly indicated by the
expression не́сколько раз:

. . . все зна́ли, что кула́к у Емелья́нова тяжёлый, не́сколько
раз ему́ пришло́сь э́то **доказа́ть.** (Тол.)
*. . . everyone knew that Yemel'yanov had a heavy fist, he had been
forced to demonstrate this several times.*

Use of the imperfective infinitive in this sentence would entail a
definite shift in meaning. It may be said that in the given context
доказа́ть = показа́ть (to show), whereas дока́зывать would lay
more emphasis on the actual process and be the equivalent of
some such verb as убежда́ть (to convince). It is interesting to note
that though the concept of repeated action makes a strong demand
for the imperfective, it nevertheless yields to lexical considerations
in cases such as this. If the imperfective infinitive were to be selected
the main verb would also be in the same aspect and the sentence
would read:

. . . не́сколько раз ему́ **приходи́лось** э́то дока́зывать.

Lastly, it should be noted that in contrast to не́сколько раз the
expression ка́ждый раз cannot be used with anything but an
imperfective.

. . . ка́ждый раз приходи́лось **дока́зывать,** что хотя́ я дейст-
ви́тельно Эренбу́рг, но всё же не не́мец. (Э.)
*. . . each time I had to show that, although I was in fact called
Erenburg, I was still not a German.*

The use of the imperfective in this case is not felt to be in contra
diction to the spirit of the sentence: as will be seen later in th
present chapter, "difficulty" is one of the concepts covered by th
imperfective infinitive. Verbs used with the expression не́сколько
раз can come under the concept of "number of completed actions"
whereas ка́ждый раз has much more explicitly a sense of "repeate
action".

(b) Habitual Action

The concept of repetitive action also includes the idea of actio
which may be habitual rather than actually put into practice on
number of occasions.

Люблю́ **ходи́ть** по алле́ям и **остана́вливаться** во́зле кио́ско
(Пау.)
I like to walk along the paths and stop at the kiosks.

Начи́танные францу́зы увлека́лись Достое́вским, от кото́рог
они́ почерпну́ли, что ру́сский лю́бит неожи́данно **убива́ть**
презира́ть де́нежные обяза́тельства, **ве́рить** в бо́га и в чёрта
оплёвывать то, во что он ве́рит, и самого́ себя́, **ка́яться**
публи́чных места́х, целу́я при э́том зе́млю. (Э.)
Well-read Frenchmen were very keen on Dostoyevskii, from whor
they learnt that a Russian loves to kill people unexpectedly, t
despise his financial commitments, to believe in God and the Devi
to spit on his beliefs and himself at the same time, and to reper
in public, kissing the ground the while.

— Он совсе́м не пил после́днее вре́мя. И всегда́ остри́л:
«Я могу́ тепе́рь то́лько накле́йки на буты́лках **прочи́ть**
вать . . .» (Кон.)
" He did not drink at all of late. And he was always joking: ' All
am fit for now is to read the labels on the bottles'."

The above sentences are true examples of "habit" in which onl
the imperfective infinitive could be used. Verbs such as люби́т

aturally introduce this concept and one will normally expect to
ind them followed by an imperfective infinitive. In the case of the
ast example it would be possible to substitute прочита́ть if the
peaker wished to say: "I can at the moment only read the la-
els . . .". This interpretation is clearly excluded by the first sen-
ence, ("of late, etc.").

When it is a question of describing "character" rather than
"habit" it becomes more a matter of subjective assessment as to
which aspect will be used. If the speaker wishes to emphasise the
wide range of circumstances in which he may act he will tend to
avour the imperfective.

Я гото́в **выполня́ть** любу́ю рабо́ту.
I am ready to carry out any sort of work.

The perfective can equally be used in a similar context where it is
esired to stress that the action will be pursued to a successful
esult.

Я гото́в **вы́полнить** любо́е зада́ние па́ртии и прави́тельства.
I am ready to carry out any task of the Party and the Govern-
ment.

In the following examples also the perfective infinitive could be
ubstituted without any appreciable change in the meaning of the
entence.

Но у неё был зави́дный хара́ктер, она́ уме́ла бы́стро **забы-**
ва́ть то, что осложня́ет жизнь. (Нек.)
But she had a character that one might well envy: she had the
ability to forget quickly anything that complicated life.

Here it would be equally correct to say она́ уме́ла бы́стро
забы́ть . . .

Она́ суме́ла забы́ть would of course once more restrict the
ct to one particular occasion. After суме́ла it would be impossible
use an imperfective infinitive.

Но не тако́в Ю́рий Андре́евич Христофо́ров, что́бы **пасова́ть**
пе́ред тру́дностями. (Вас.)
*But Yurii Andreyevich Khristoforov was not the kind of man to
give up in front of difficulties.*

(пасова́ть/спасова́ть: lit. *to pass in card games*).

Here the usage is purely optional; there is in fact a tendency to
follow что́бы with a perfective infinitive even when it has a general
application, as in this sentence.

(c) Rule of Conduct

With examples such as that quoted above the idea of habitual
action merges into that of general principles formulated to guide
the speaker or another party.

Всё всегда́ на́до **принима́ть** так, как оно́ прихо́дит. (Кон.)
You always have to take everything as it comes.
— За таки́е шту́ки на́до мора́льно **убива́ть** . . . (Акс.)
"For things like that people ought to be made moral outcasts . . .
— Я не должна́ **предупрежда́ть** ка́ждого рабо́чего. (Ант.)
"It is not up to me to warn every worker individually."
Уж е́сли и **выходи́ть** за́муж, то за челове́ка, кото́рый потя́нет
вперёд . . . (Ант.)
*If I am going to get married at all then it will be to a man who will
pull me on in life.*
— Ива́н, — сказа́л Андре́й. — Прошу́ тебя́ никогда́ ко мне
не **приходи́ть.** (Ол.)
"Ivan," said Andrei, "I beg you never to come to see me."
Ты хо́чешь научи́ть меня́ **подчиня́ться** тебе́ беспрекосло́вно?
(Оку.)
You want to train me to submit to you unquestioningly?
Охладе́вший во́здух, каза́лось, ну́жно бы́ло **razлива́ть** по
буты́лкам, что́бы **вози́ть** в го́род и что́бы там, хотя́ бы в
таки́х до́зах, всё же принима́ли его́ городски́е лю́ди. (Сол.)

One felt as though one should pour the cool air into bottles to bring it into town and let the townspeople drink it there, even if they only got such small doses of it.

As will be seen in the next section on the perfective there is a strong tendency to use a perfective infinitive with мочь/можно and должен, etc. Note, however, the following examples:

«... мо́жно ли руководи́телю **проявля́ть** инициати́ву в аплодисме́нтах?» (Вас.)
"... is it permissible for a manager to take the lead in starting the clapping?"

Но большо́е что́-то **де́лать,** во всю свою́ си́лу, до́лжен я обяза́тельно: ре́ки ли **запира́ть,** го́ры ли **передвига́ть** ... (Сар.)
But I must do something big without fail, and put all my strength into it, whether it be blocking up rivers or moving mountains ...

запира́ть/запере́ть: lit. *to lock*).

Only in these last two examples would it be possible to substitute perfective infinitives; in all the other sentences quoted above the imperfective would be the only possible usage.

As has already been seen in the case of the imperative the imperfective is frequently used in the case of public notices which have the force of a general instruction. In the example given below it would of course be impossible to use perfective infinitives.

Воспреща́ется: **бежа́ть** по зскала́тору, **сади́ться,** и **ста́вить** ве́щи на ступе́ни. (Notice in underground station.)
It is forbidden to run on the escalator, to sit down or to place articles on the steps.

Note that in the case of the double imperfective verb бе́гать/бежа́ть the determinate infinitive is here favoured, as бе́гать would imply not only "to run on various occasions", but also "in various directions".

The infinitive can be used with a similar "imperative" force in radio signals, etc.

В слу́чае серьёзных ава́рий экипа́жам **выходи́ть** на лёд. (Кон.)

In the case of serious damage crews are to get out on the ice.

(2) Continuous Action

Action in progress may be clearly indicated by some such expression as це́лый день, всю неде́лю.

Це́лый день **по́лзать** по жаре́ и́з-за парши́вых ка́мешков. (Наг.)

To think we shall have to crawl round in the heat all day because of these wretched stones.

(ка́мешек — diminutive of ка́мень.)

The concept of continuous action also emerges quite distinctly in those cases where an imperfective infinitive is contrasted, so to speak, with a "narrative" action in the perfective. Compare the switch of aspects in the following example.

Из До́ма торго́вли он прошёл в большо́й «гастроно́м» на Не́вском. Здесь он совсе́м потеря́л го́лову, так захоте́лось ему́ **встать** за прила́вок, **ре́зать** колба́сы, **отве́шивать** сёмгу

From the Main Store he passed on to a big food shop on the Nevskii Prospect. Here he completely lost his head: he was seized by such a desire to take up his own place behind the counter, to cut up the sausages and weigh out the salmon.

It is not difficult to imagine the same phrase in the past tense with these aspects used to express "he took his place behind the counter" (встал — perfective) and "he was cutting up sausages and weighing out salmon" (ре́зал . . . отве́шивал — imperfective).

In many other cases the idea of continuous action is simply expressed by the choice of the imperfective aspect for the infinitive

Каки́е бы счёты ещё ни пришло́сь **своди́ть** по́сле войны́ . . .
(Сим.)
*However many other scores we may still have to settle after
the war.*

In this case the speaker views the settling of accounts as a long
process which will not readily be brought to an end. Examples such
as this might equally well be classified under the category of
"process rather than result".

(3) Uncompleted Action

(a) Attempted Action

The imperfective infinitive will often be used when the action
in question has not been brought to a successful conclusion.

Я хоте́л **уходи́ть,** но Влади́мир Ильи́ч меня́ удержа́л. (Э.)
I wanted to leave, but Vladimir Il'ich made me stay.

хоте́л here has really the force of "tried" and the past tense of
хоте́ть can frequently be thus translated

На́до бы́ло что́-то **предпринима́ть.** (Вас.)
It was necessary to try something.

Perfective infinitives (уйти́ and предприня́ть) would also be
possible in both these sentences and would give an idea of greater
urgency and resolution.

Они́ реши́ли, кто здоро́вые, осо́бенно из нача́льства, сего́дня
к но́чи у Се́верной ба́лки вдоль лима́на **пробива́ться.** Они́
но́чью ата́ку там ду́мают сде́лать. (Сим.)
*They have decided that those among them who are fit, especially
the officers, will try to break out by nightfall along the estuary
by the North Ravine. They are intending to make an attack there
in the night.*

пробиться as a verb which is strongly terminative in character will frequently have this sense of "attempted action" whenever it is used in the imperfective.

As we have seen in the chapters on the indicative there is sometimes a contrast between an action in progress (impf.) and another action which interrupts it (perf.) A similar usage can be seen clearly with the imperfective infinitive.

Нужно было **проходить** через двор. В это время из подъезда, куда её вели, вышел кудрявый юноша . . . (Тол.)
They had to go through the yard. At that moment from the door to which she was being led emerged a curly-headed young man . . .

(b) Influence of the Negative Modifying the Infinitive Directly

The negative may modify either the finite verb or the infinitive itself. This latter case is comparatively simple, as the infinitive is reflecting a negative aspect. Generally some such word as просьба is understood.

Дверью не **хлопать**.
Do not slam the door.

В зале не **разговаривать**.
No talking in the room.

In other cases the request is made more explicit by the insertion of a verb such as просить.

И прошу не **перебивать**.
And I beg you not to interrupt.

И прошу тебя не **изворачиваться**. (Роз.)
And I ask you not to try and evade the issue.

Сколько раз я вас просила ничего ему не **заказывать**? (Вас.)
How many times have I asked you not to order anything from him?

Панин: . . . Только давайте уговоримся: где приказал стоять, там и стойте. За мной не **ездить**. (Сим.)
Panin: . . . Only let us get this settled: wherever I order you to stop, there you are to stay. You are not to drive after me.

The negative generally calls for an imperfective infinitive after other expressions besides requests and orders.

Однако он не сказал ни слова, он вообще решил не **вмешиваться** — то было не его, а её прошлое. (Казв.)
However, he did not say a word, he had decided to refrain completely from interfering—it was her past and not his.
— А вы как решили с экзаменами?
— Мы решили не **поступать**. (Акс.)
"And what did you decide about the examinations?"
"We decided not to go in for them."

(c) Negative with Finite Verb

The most important factor determining the aspect of the infinitive is the verb or expression preceding it. Most of the auxiliaries tend to be followed by a perfective infinitive.

Я хочу **увидеть** его. Я могу это **сделать**. Я постараюсь тебе **позвонить**.
I want to see him. I can do that. I will try to phone you.

Similarly most of the expressions governing the infinitive tend to place it in the perfective aspect.

Ты должен **прийти** точно в семь. Нужно будет его **предупредить**. Можно **войти**?
You must come sharp on seven. It will be necessary to warn him. May I come in?

These usages and the exceptions to them will therefore be examined under the section on the perfective. There are, however, two large groups of expressions with a negative sense which are followed by an imperfective infinitive and which merit attention at this point.

(i) "I do not want . . ." and cognate expressions.

Я не хочу **оставаться** с вами. (Сим.)
I don't want to stay with you.

Уезжа́ть за грани́цу мне не хоте́лось: всё, чем я жил бы́ло в Росси́и. (Э.)
I did not want to go abroad: all my interests in life were in Russia.

Similarly when жела́ть is used with a negative:

Ва́ся, не жела́я **выдава́ть** свои́х пережива́ний. . . (Вас.)
Vasya, not wanting to show what he had been through. . .

Further idioms expressing unwillingness or reluctance are also followed by an imperfective infinitive.

Но бы́ло **лень** встава́ть. (Казв.)
But they felt too lazy to get up.

Охо́та тебе́ вы́говор выслу́шивать. (Вас.)
Do you really like being told off?

Хва́тит мне разы́грывать вас.
I have done enough playing jokes on you.

Чёрт с тобо́й. **Не охо́та** свя́зываться . . . Вре́мени у меня́ в обре́з. (Вас.)
Devil take you. I don't want to get caught up with you. I'm very pushed for time.

— **Неуже́ли** тащи́ть домо́й? Ра́зве нельзя́ купи́ть другу́ю? (Ол.)
"Do I really have to drag it home with me? Is it impossible to buy another one?"

— А как же, — говори́т Ка́рпов, — вперёд идём, ребя́та. **Хва́тит** отси́живаться. (Оку.)
"Well, boys," says Karpov, "we are starting an advance. We have done enough sitting about."

Я **не собира́юсь** теря́ть фо́рму и́з-за како́го-то психопа́та. (Акс.)
I have no intention of getting worked up over some madman or other.

— Слу́шай, де́тка. Ди́мка нахму́рился. Хочу́ предупреди́ть . . .
Конча́й, зна́ешь, свои́ закидо́ны (pop.) гла́зками и про́чие
шу́ры-му́ры (pop.). Мы **не собира́емся** тут за тебя́ ка́шу
расхлёбывать. (Акс.)
"Listen, my child." Dimka frowned. "I want to warn you . . .
Give over all this making sheep's eyes at men and this sort of
fooling about. We have no intention of straightening things out
after you."

(Contrast the use of the perfective infinitive when the negative
is omitted.

А ещё актри́сой собира́ешься **стать.** (Акс.)
And what is more, you are setting out to be an actress.)

— Вы бы вот подсказа́ли нача́льству . . .
— **Что мне** подска́зывать? Я для тебя́ сам нача́льство.
(Ант.)
" You ought to suggest to the people in charge . . ."
" What do you mean 'I ought to suggest'? I am the one in charge
of you."

(ii) "You should not . . ." and cognate expressions.

На́до has two parallel meanings, according to whether it implies
a necessity imposed by physical circumstances or one which is the
equivalent of an order. When used without a negative this distinction has no practical importance: in both senses на́до will be followed by a perfective infinitive.

1. Снег идёт: на́до **закры́ть** окно́.
It is snowing. We must shut the window.

2. Мне на́до за́втра **офо́рмить** вид на жи́тельство.
I have to put my residence permit in order tomorrow.

Не на́до has most frequently the second of these two meanings;
that is to say it is used to dissuade someone from an action they
may be about to undertake.

Не на́до э́того **де́лать.** Он поймёт и без э́того.
You should not do that. He will understand without that.

In this usage не на́до is followed by the imperfective aspects of the infinitive.

Не на́до will occasionally be found also in the sense that there is no necessity for a certain action.

Не на́до туда́ **е́хать** до семи́ часо́в. Мы и так доста́нем биле́ты.
It is not necessary to go there before seven o'clock. We will get tickets even then.

(и так — *all the same*)

Even in cases such as this the sense of inadvisability is felt to predominate and an imperfective infinitive is used.

Нельзя́ on the other hand gives a contrast between dissuasion or the forbidding of an action as against impossibility.

Нельзя́ **ходи́ть** по газо́нам. *Keep off the grass.*

Нельзя́ **выступа́ть** на э́том собра́нии.
You should not speak at that meeting.

Нельзя́ **вы́учить** всё э́то за неде́лю.
You cannot learn all this in a week.

Here we see two broad categories emerging; dissuasion: imperfective infinitive, and impossibility: perfective infinitive.

Contrast:

Нельзя́ туда́ **входи́ть.**
You are not allowed in there.

with:

Туда́ нельзя́ **войти́.**
It is impossible to get in there. (i.e. because the door is locked, there are too many people, etc.)

Belevitskaya* lists the following expressions as being used to dissuade someone from undertaking or completing a given action:

* Ру́сский язы́к для студе́нтов-иностра́нцев, МГУ, 1959, p. 99. Several ples have been drawn from the same article.

Не на́до, не име́ет смы́сла, не сто́ит, не сле́дует, хва́тит, дово́льно, доста́точно, не́зачем, не́чего, не́ к чему.

Не́ на́до заступа́ться за меня́. Я сам отве́чу за свои́ оши́бки.
You don't have to stick up for me. I will answer for my own mistakes.

Хва́тит, говори́т, мяч гоня́ть (Акс.)
"That's enough kicking the ball about," he says.

— . . . на́шему бра́ту **не поло́жено** выбира́ть. (Вор.)
. . . it's not for the likes of us to choose.

When the expressions convey the idea: "there is no use/no need to", they are also followed by an imperfective infinitive.

Не́ к чему с ним разгова́ривать, он всё равно́ не поймёт.
There is no point talking to him, he will not understand anything anyway.

Не́ за что меня́ благодари́ть.
There is nothing to thank me for.

Не́чего на́до мной смея́ться.
There is no reason to laugh at me.

On the other hand if expressions of this group do not carry the idea of dissuasion the aspect of the infinitive will depend on whether the action in question has a general application or is limited to one particular instance.

Мне не́ к чему **прислони́ться.**
I have nothing to lean against (*now*—perf.)
В авто́бусе не́ к чему **прислоня́ться.**
There is nothing to lean against in the bus (on an unspecified number of occasions—imperf.)

The number of expressions used to restrain someone from an action is enormous. A sample of them will be found in the examples which follow.

Как ты сме́ешь возража́ть про́тив того́, что у меня́ живёт еди́нственный мой друг? (Сим.)

How can you dare to object to my only friend living with me?

Нельзя́ безнака́занно в тече́ние трёх и́ли четырёх лет пред-почита́ть стихи́ говя́дине. (Э.)

One cannot with impunity forsake meat (lit. *beef*) *for poetry over the course of three or four years.*

(Note that though the verb *to be able* has been introduced into the English translation it signifies in this sentence "inadvisability" rather than physical impossibility, hence the imperfective infinitive.)

Лу́чше не обостря́ть отноше́ний. (Роз.)

It would be better not to embitter relations.

Как ты сме́ешь презира́ть мою́ жизнь?

How dare you despise my life?

Де́лать не́чего, и ничего́ **не на́до** де́лать. (Акс.)

There is nothing to do and it is not necessary to do anything.

На́до только́ **не** зарыва́ться. (Вас.)

All that matters is not to go to extremes.

Абсолю́тно ни о чём **нельзя́** бы́ло расска́зывать. (Акс.)

It was inadvisable for him to tell about any of this.

Что же я вам э́то говорю́? Вы-то его́ зна́ете, **не мне** вам расска́зывать . . . (Казв.)

Why do I have to say this to you? You know him after all, I don't need to tell you about him.

Хозя́ин поражён как нельзя́ бо́льше, но уде́рживать его́ коне́чно, **не сме́ет.** (Бун.)

His host is extremely astonished, but of course does not dare to detain him.

Упаси́ вас бог при посети́теле самому́ абоне́нта вызыва́ть. (Вас.)

God forbid that when a visitor is there he should see you trying to get through to someone yourself (i.e. *an underling should 'phone for you.*)

(абонéнт — subscriber)

И запóмни, что здесь обижáть тебя́ **я не позвóлю** никомý, дáже сы́ну. (Сим.)

And remember that I will not allow anyone to insult you here, not even my son.

Старикá обижáть никомý **не позвóлю**. (Сим.)

I will not allow anyone to offend the old man.

... а **глáвное** не напивáться — ты пóмнишь, как я заболéл?

... but the most important thing is not to drink too much—you remember how ill I was.

When, however, the expressions не нáдо, etc. are in a context which implied that the action should in fact be undertaken the infinitive naturally reverts to the perfective. Such meanings are frequently found in the form of rhetorical questions.

Не нáдо ли вам тудá **пойти́?**

Do you not think that you ought to go there?

(Which we may contrast with:

Не нáдо вам тудá **идти́.**

You ought not to go there.)

(4) Process Stressed rather than Result

(a) Verbs which must be Followed by the Imperfective Infinitive

One of the few firm rules in the handling of the aspects is that verbs meaning *to begin/continue/finish* are followed by an infinitive in the imperfective aspect.

Начинáть/начáть, кончáть/кóнчить, стать, продолжáть/продóлжить, приступáть/приступи́ть, принимáться/приня́ться, брáться/взя́ться, переставáть/перестáть, бросáть/брóсить.

Он ко́нчил **петь**.
He finished singing.

Он не стал ему́ **возража́ть**.
He did not start to argue with him.

Челове́к на у́лице продолжа́ет **восклица́ть,** но не́сколько
ти́ше: — Отчего́ ты молчи́шь? Я пришёл тебе́ сообщи́ть
но́вость . . . (Ол.)
*The man standing in the street goes on exlaiming, though not so
loudly: "Why won't you speak? I've come to tell you some news . . ."*

Note too the verbs in the examples below which are also normally constructed with the imperfective infinitive.

Он **привы́к** кури́ть (привыка́ть/привы́кнуть).
He acquired the habit of smoking.

Ему́ **запрети́ли** кури́ть (запреща́ть/запрети́ть).
He was forbidden to smoke.

Мне **надое́ло** напомина́ть тебе́ об э́том (надоеда́ть/надое́сть).
I am tired of reminding you about this.

Я **уста́л** игра́ть (устава́ть/уста́ть).
I am tired of playing.

Она́ **учи́лась** гото́вить (учи́ться/вы́учиться).
She learnt to cook.

(b) Adverbs Modifying the Infinitive Directly

Он реши́л не **встреча́ться** с Сюза́нной, пока́ не бу́дет гото́ва
э́та ро́за. (Пау.)
He decided not to meet Suzanna until this rose was ready.

Not only the negative, but adverbs in general tend to be used with
an imperfective infinitive. First we may study the cases where the
adverb modifies the infinitive itself. Those expressions which enforce an imperfective in the indicative (listed on p. 40) will naturally also require its use in the infinitive.

Нам пришло́сь его́ до́лго **ждать.**
We had to wait for him for a long time.

На́до **писа́ть** заявле́ние ка́ждый раз, когда́ хо́чешь приня́ть
го́стя в общежи́тии.
*You have to write out an application every time you want to bring
a guest into the hostel.*

Ему́ бы поча́ще **ви́деться** с ней.
He ought to see her more often.

Adverbs and adverbial phrases such as these necessarily imply
he concepts of repetitive action or action in progress which have
een dealt with at the beginning of the present chapter. Belevits-
aya quotes two useful examples.

На́до ча́ще **загля́дывать** в слова́рь.
You will have to refer more often to the dictionary.

ча́ще modifies the infinitive, hence imperfective.

Ча́сто, что́бы вспо́мнить значе́ние сло́ва, на́до **загляну́ть**
в слова́рь.
*Often in order to recall the meaning of a word one has to look it
up in the dictionary.*

ча́сто is not linked directly with the infinitive which remains in
he perfective, as is normal after на́до.

Even those adverbs which imply that the action should be carried
ut speedily tend to be followed by an imperfective infinitive. This
logical if one considers that they are drawing attention to the
anner of executing the action and hence to the idea of "process".

Респу́блика име́ет возмо́жности ре́зко **увели́чивать** произ-
во́дство хло́пка. (МР.)
*It is possible for the Republic to achieve a sharp rise in the pro-
duction of cotton.*

— К чёрту! На́до скоре́й **переходи́ть** в инжене́ры. (Вор.)
"To the devil with it! I must make a quick transfer to the engineers."

Все торопи́лись, все должны́ бы́ли вот-вот **уходи́ть** в мо́ре (Кон.)
They were all hurrying, they all had to put out to sea in a very short while.

(c) Adverbs Modifying the Finite Verb

Where the main verb is modified by an adverb implying repetitive or long-continuing action this effect is generally carried over into the aspect of the infinitive.

Он ча́сто хотел **ви́деться** с ней, а всё же не пое́хал в Ленинград.
He often wanted to see her, yet did not go to Leningrad.

(d) Difficulty, Doubt, Hesitation, etc.

Very frequently what Russian grammarians give as an adverb is the equivalent in English of a sentence containing the words "it is"/"it was" etc. In such instances almost any emotional over tone in the "adverb" may lead the speaker to use an imperfective infinitive.

Всем ка́к-то со́вестно **уходи́ть** отсю́да, **возвраща́ться** на су́дно . . . (Кон.)
Somehow they all felt twinges of conscience at leaving here and going back onto the boat.

А то уже́ бо́льно оби́дно **помира́ть** бы́ло. (Сим.)
Otherwise it would go terribly against the grain to die.

Юрочке бы́ло ка́к-то нело́вко **знако́мить** их. (Нек.)
Yurochka felt somehow embarrassed about introducing them to each other.

Заче́м е́хать туда́? Че́рез год **возвраща́ться** — неудо́бно (Гла.)
Why should I go there? To try to come back after a year would be awkward.

Sentences of this sort are almost identical with the idea of "reluctance" expressed on pp. 115–117. Similar usages occur with those that give the idea of "difficulty".

Там, в тайге, за тридцать тысяч километров будет поздно от меня **освобождаться.** (Вор.)
It will be too late to get rid of me when we are thirty thousand kilometres away in the forest.

Мне смешно даже **равняться** с ними. (Гла.)
It is ridiculous for me even to try to compare myself with them.

А потом подумаю: откуда **вспоминать** начало? (Сим.)
And then the thought comes into my mind (N.B. future): *how can I remember the beginning?*

Curiously enough the word трудно itself is generally followed by a perfective infinitve.

Добраться до Мёртвой бухты было трудно. (Пау.)
It was difficult to get as far as Dead Bay.

In the case of трудно the impossibility of completing the action is stressed (cf. нельзя in the sense of *it is impossible*).

Черты лица **различить** трудно. Лицо в пыли и с чёрными полосами машинного масла. (Гла.)
It is difficult to make out the features of his face. His face is covered with dust and black stripes of motor oil.

) Idea of Process Contained in Infinitive without Adverb

The imperfective infinitive will often occur to express an underlying feeling that one is faced with a long and possibly complicated task.

Олеша пошёл вместе со мной по пустым коридорам гостиницы **выбирать** самую лучшую комнату. (Пау.)
Olyesha set off with me along the empty corridors of the hotel to choose the best room.

Перезимова́в у Со́ни, Ла́тышев в полово́дье пришёл сно́ва **нанима́ться** на спаса́тельную ста́нцию. Его́ по́дняли на смех . . . (Вас.)

*Latyshev spent the winter at Sonya's place and in the time of the
spring floods came to seek employment again at the life-guard
station. They laughed him to scorn . . .*

— И винт **меня́ть** на́до, — сказа́л меха́ник. (Кон.)

" And we will have to change the propeller", said the mechanic.

— . . . у тебя́ четы́ре ря́да **перекла́дывать.** (Ант.)

. . . "you will have four courses (of brickwork) to lay again."

— Мне на́до **уходи́ть,** — сказа́л Во́льнов, и сухо́й язы́к пло́хо слу́шался его́. (Кон.)

*" I have to go," said Vol'nov and his dry tongue was not completely
under control.*

A feeling of reluctance can also be conveyed simply by the use
of an imperfective infinitive without any adverb.

На́до бы́ло **возвраща́ться** на су́дно, на ма́ленький коря́вый се́йнер. (Кон.)

*They had to go back to the ship, onto the little ungainly seine
fishing boat.*

Ideas of hesitation are also contained in this usage.

Че́рез не́сколько мину́т я могу́ нача́ть свой о́пыт. На́до **начина́ть,** чего́ там ду́мать. (Акс.)

*After a few minutes I can begin my experiment. I must get started
there can be no second thoughts about it.*

Как я смогу́ **защища́ть** диссерта́цию, е́сли узна́ю сего́дня что вы́воды непра́вильные. (Акс.)

*How will I be able to defend my thesis if I find out to-day that m
conclusions are incorrect?*

If it were not for the idea of difficulty in the speaker's mind on
would normally expect to find a perfective infinitive after th
verb смочь.

To lay stress on the idea of process the imperfective aspect can be used even after expressions which normally have a strong tendency to take the perfective.

Пришлось **разыскивать** знакомых, не связанных с подпольем. (Э.)
I had to seek out people I knew who were not connected with the underground.

Я попробовал **перестукиваться** — никто не ответил. (Э.)
I tried tapping out a message to my neighbour—no-one answered.

Ты увидишь, это поможет тебе **выполнять** план.
You will see—this will help you to fulfil the plan.

Compare also the change of aspect in the following examples:

И доказали этим своё преимущество и своё право на то, чтобы **перестраивать** Европу. (Сим.)
And they have proved their superiority by this and their right to refashion Europe.

The speaker is thinking of the reconstruction as a long and possibly complicated process. Later, on the same page, another speaker tends to mock at the idea and uses the perfective infinitive with a touch of sarcasm which is reinforced by the word просто.

Нет, мы тут без тебя просто собирались **перестроить** Европу. (Сим.)
No, while you were out we were just getting ready to rebuild Europe.

— Из-за этого-то надо бросать жену с ребёнком? Вы должны **перевоспитать** и жену, и отца её, и мать — всех! (Тен.)
"Was it necessary because of this to abandon your wife and child? You must re-educate both your wife and her father and her mother—all of them . . ."

Here the party secretary considers that the result can easily be obtained; when later she puts the idea in the form of a question she is already tending to think of it more as a process.

Ну уж ... Са́мое позо́рное, что мо́жно предста́вить — э́то расписа́ться в со́бственном бесси́лии. Вы про́бовали их **перевоспи́тывать**? (Тен.)

This is the most shameful thing one can imagine—to sign a certificate of one's own helplessness. Have you tried to re-educate them?

A similar idea of difficulty accounts for the change to the imperfective infinitive in the following example:

— Ты мне не ве́ришь?

— Не ве́рю.

— Как мне тебе́ **доказа́ть**?

— До́каза́ть? Ты собира́ешься **дока́зывать**? (Акс.)

" *You do not believe me?*"

"*I don't.*"

" *How can I prove it to you?*"

" *Prove it? You are going to prove it?*"

(f) The Infinitive after Verbs of Motion

When the verb stands in the present the tendency seems to be to regard the infinitive as expressing a process which the subject is about to embark on and to use the imperfective aspect. Perfective infinitives are also possible but not so common.

Он идёт **раздева́ться** (**мыть** руки и т. п.)

He goes to take off his coat (wash his hands, etc.)

This form is used for stage directions in plays. In everyday speech the past is often heard and with it either infinitive can be used.

— Куда́ он пошёл?

— Он пошёл **откры́ть** (**открыва́ть**) дверь.

" *Where has he gone?*"

" *He has gone to open the door.*"

The same pairing of the aspects normally occurs with the other verbs "to go" (not on foot).

Она́ пое́хала **встреча́ть/встре́тить** его́.
She has gone to meet him.
Она́ пое́хала **покупа́ть/купи́ть** биле́ты.
She has gone to buy the tickets.

In the second example the perfective is rarely used. It seems that unless one is specifying very exactly the object in question with, this particular combination the imperfective infinitive is generally preferred. Note, however, that with уе́хать the perfective is also possible.

Она́ уе́хала **купи́ть** биле́ты.
She has gone off to buy the tickets.

Spagis (p. 378) points out that either aspect of the infinitive can be used after verbs "to go" except where a time limit is implied (зае́хать/зайти́: *to call in—and go out again*), or stated by some such expression as на мину́тку.) She quotes as examples:

Я зае́хал **прости́ться** с тобо́й.
I looked in to say good-bye to you.
Он вы́шел на у́лицу **подыша́ть** све́жим во́здухом.
He went outside to get a breath of fresh air.
Гром прокати́лся где́-то бли́зко и предостерега́юще, в ко́мнату пахну́ло ве́тром, и я поспеши́л **затвори́ть** о́кна . . . (Бун.)
Somewhere close at hand there was a warning peal of thunder, a gust of wind swept into the room and I hastened to close the windows.

B. PERFECTIVE ASPECT

1) Desire

a) Applying to One Occasion

When the verb "to wish" relates to a particular instance, naturally the perfective infinitive is favoured.

Ма́ма, я хочу́ **взять** э́то с собо́й в парк сего́дня.
Mother, I want to take it with me to the park today.

Of course this concept is over-ruled in the case of verbs which
have no true aspectual pair. This occurs particularly with "durative" verbs where the gap between the meanings of the aspects is
generally wider than in the case of "terminative" verbs.

Мне **пить** хо́чется.   Я хочу́ **игра́ть** сего́дня.
Now I am thirsty.   *I want to play today.*

Similarly after verbs "to try" etc.:

Он лови́л себя́ на том, что стара́лся **каза́ться** грубе́е и
мужчи́нистее, не́жели был на са́мом де́ле. (Кон.)
He caught himself trying to seem ruder and more masculine than
he really was.

The corresponding perfectives have the following meanings:

вы́пить: *drink* (alcohol); сыгра́ть: *play* (not absolute); пока-
за́ться: either *appear in view*, or *seem* (implying that an illusion
is involved).

(b) Repetitive and Habitual

Even when their effect is applied to a number of occasions, verbs
such as хоте́ть and жела́ть tend to be followed by a perfective
infinitive.

Почему́-то он всегда́ заболева́л в пе́рвый день кани́кул.
Он хоте́л **вы́здороветь,** но не мог. (Гла.)
For some reason or other he always used to fall ill on the first day
of the holidays. He wanted to get better, but could not.

Although the verbs "to desire" can be followed by a perfective
infinitive even when this has a general application, if the concept
of repetitive action is explicitly stated the imperfective must be
used.

Я хочу́ ви́деть его́ **ка́ждый понеде́льник.**
I want to see him every Monday.

Я хочу́ купа́ться **как мо́жно ча́ще** до отъе́зда.
I want to bathe as often as possible before I go away.

It would be impossible where expressions of this type (ка́ждый [ра]з/день, ча́сто) occur to substitute perfective infinitives. If the [ex]pressions indicating repetition were not included, in both these [se]ntences it would be possible to have the infinitive in either aspect [w]ith no real distinction in meaning between the two aspects.

Я хочу́ **ви́деть/уви́деть** его́ за́втра.
I want to see him tomorrow.

Я хочу́ **купа́ться/вы́купаться** сего́дня.
I want to bathe today.

This is yet another instance of the wider range of meaning of the [im]perfective.

Refusal

Notwithstanding what has been said in the first half of this chap[te]r on the use of не хочу́, etc. with the imperfective infinitive, when [th]ese negatives are used to express not merely reluctance, but a [ca]tegorical decision, they may be followed by the infinitive in the [pe]rfective.

Contrast the following pair of sentences:

[Im]perfective	Perfective
[Я] не хочу́ здесь **остава́ться.**	Я не хочу́ **оста́ться** здесь.
[I d]o not want to stay here	*I do not want to stay here*
[i.]e. I would sooner go some-	*(almost equivalent to: I simply*
[wh]ere else).	*will not stay here).*

Although the perfective infinitive will follow negative verbs of [de]sire only in a small proportion of cases, this usage will occasion[all]y be found in cases where a strong will power is exercised [ag]ainst committing a certain action.

Или он из упря́мства, из самолю́бия не хо́чет тепе́рь **пока**-
за́ть всем, что его́ ошеломи́л побе́г Ба́укина. (Нил.)

Or perhaps from stubbornness or a sense of pride he does no
want at present to show to everyone that he was shaken by Baukin
flight.

Он да́же намека́л на свою́ дру́жбу с ни́ми, во что мы ника́
не могли́ пове́рить. Верне́е не хоте́ли **пове́рить.** (Нил.)

He even hinted at his friendship with them, which we simply cou
not believe in. It would be truer to say that we refused to belie
in it.

(d) Infinitive expressing Desire without Auxiliary Verb

Unless the concept of repetition is given special emphasis th
construction is normally found with the perfective.

Мы обе́дали, я не́рвничал, гляде́л на часы́ — не **опозда́ть** бы
(Э.)

We were having dinner; I was worried and was looking at n
watch—we must not be late.

Но то́лько бы **добра́ться** до тайги́. (Вор.)

But if only I could get as far as the forest.

(тайга́ — *Siberian forest*)

Similar constructions are sometimes found with the verb ду́мат

И она́ уже́ ду́мает, как бы **дожи́ть** до миха́йлова дня. (Каз*
And she is already thinking how she can live through to St. Michae
day.

(e) Attempted Action

In this case one always hopes to bring the action to a successf
conclusion. It seems natural therefore for the infinitives to
placed in the perfective aspect.

Поздне́е мы втроём пыта́лись **сде́лать** то же, и ничего́ у н
не получи́лось. (Вор.)

Later the three of us tried to do the same thing and could r
manage to do anything.

Бори́с Леони́дович пыта́лся **убеди́ть** перево́дчика не публикова́ть перево́дов не́которых его́ ста́рых произведе́ний.
Boris Leonidovich tried to persuade the translator not to publish the translations of some of his earlier works.

In both the above examples the main verb (пыта́ться) is in the imperfective, expressing the fact that the action was undertaken over a period of time or on a number of occasions. In neither case was the attempt successful; nevertheless the infinitive refers to an action which the persons concerned wanted to complete and therefore the perfective is selected.

However, if the idea of repetition is felt to be important the imperfective can also be used.

Ве́тер обдува́ет ка́пли на стекле́. Они́ стека́ют ко́со. И ка́ждая стара́ется **скользи́ть** по сле́ду предыду́щей, по уже́ мо́крой, ско́льзкой доро́жке. (Кон.)
The wind is blowing round the drops on the glass. They stream down slant-wise and each of them tries to slide down the track of the one before, a path which is already wet and slippery.

Obviously similar expressions will follow the same pattern even the attempt was not actually initiated.

Когда́ Слепцо́в прости́лся и собра́лся уйти́, Виноку́ров гото́в был **уда́рить** свою́ жену́ по лицу́. (Казч.)
When Sleptsov had taken his leave and got ready to go, Vinokurov was in such a state that he could have hit his wife in the face.

Она́ сде́лала уси́лие **поня́ть** — что он говори́т. Кака́я-то насто́йчивая мысль меша́ла ей сосредото́читься. (Тол.)
She made an effort to understand what he was saying. Some insistent thought prevented her from concentrating.

Поле́сов собира́лся бы́ло уже́ **возврати́ться** в мастерску́ю . . . (Ильф.)

Polesov was already on the point of going back into the work
shop . . .

бы́ло in this usage implies that the intended action was in fac
never carried out (cf. хоте́л бы́ло, p. 54).

Он, пра́вда, рискну́л, отъедини́вшись от толпы́, **перебра́тьс**
за верёвку, огражда́ющую по́дступы к труби́не. (Ол.)
It was true that he dared to separate himself from the crowd an.
to get past the rope which cordoned off the steps to the platforn.

(f) Fear

Even with the negative of such verbs as рискну́ть in the las
example the perfective infinitive is normally found. Such expression
often have the force of "to be afraid".

Парохо́д да́же заме́длил ход, как бы не реша́ясь **потрево́жит**
э́ту светоно́сную о́бласть земли́. (Пау.)
The steamer even slowed down, as though it could not make up it
mind to disturb this radiant region of the earth.

In a sentence such as this it would only be possible to substitut
an imperfective infinitive if repetitive action was implied (i.e. "o
every occasion it passed this way it did not dare . . ."). In case
where some idea of "fear" is implied it seems to be normal t
throw the stress on to the fact that one is afraid to carry out th
action in each *individual* instance, or that the misfortune wi
occur at some given moment.

Васи́лий мо́лча хлеба́л суп, боя́сь **взгляну́ть.** (Казв.)
Vasilii was silently supping his soup, afraid to look up.
Лю́ся оста́лась в Москве́. И тебе́ стра́шно её **потеря́ть.** (Гла
Lyusya has remained in Moscow. And you are terrified of losin.
her.
Ничего́ они́ в жи́зни не боя́лись. Ничего́ не боя́лись **потеря́т**
(Гла.)
They feared nothing in life. There was nothing they feared to los.

Although it might be thought that the concept of "fear" would be close to that of "reluctance" (with imperfective infinitive), in practice бояться and similar expressions seem to follow the same tendency as стараться (see section (e) of this chapter), and are almost always found with perfective infinitives.

g) Purpose

Infinitives constructed with чтобы are perfective in the vast majority of cases. Spagis gives examples:

Мы ка́ждое у́тро открыва́ли окно́, чтобы **прове́трить** ко́мнату.
We used to open the window every morning to air the room.

Поднима́ясь на́ гору, мы не́сколько раз останавливались, чтобы **отдохну́ть.**
Going uphill, we stopped several times to rest.

It is possible in rare cases to use the imperfective to stress the fact that action the was long-lasting or continuous.

Что́бы **обеспе́чивать** постоя́нное снабже́ние пи́щей . . .
In order to ensure a constant supply of food . . .

2) Possibility

a) "To be Able" etc.

The verb мочь and expressions such as мо́жно, быть в состоя́нии, which have similar force, can in many cases be constructed with an imperfective infinitive.

Не могу́ бо́льше **скрыва́ть** от вас . . .
I can no longer hide from you . . .

Он тепе́рь не мог бы с ни́ми **разгова́ривать** и да́же на них **смотре́ть** (Казч.)
He could not now have talked with them, or even looked at them.

The first example is complicated by the introduction of the expression бо́льше ... не, which implies that an action which was hitherto continuous has now been broken off. The second example must have imperfective infinitives, since there are no true perfective pairs for the verbs разгова́ривать and смотре́ть. In both examples it may be felt that не мочь is almost the equivalent of the expressions denoting "reluctance", which have been noted in the first half of this chapter, (pp. 115–117) as taking the imperfective infinitive.

Similarly when мочь has a force equivalent to уме́ть it will obviously be followed by an imperfective infinitive: here we are dealing with an ability which has general application and is not restricted to one particular instance.

Я могу́ о́чень бы́стро **бе́гать.**
I can run very fast.

Я могу́ **чита́ть** англи́йские кни́ги без словаря́.
I can read English books without a dictionary.

A distinction can also be drawn sometimes between a rule with general applicability or permission given for one occasion only. Compare:

Imperfective	Perfective
Вы мо́жете **по́льзоваться** телефо́ном. *You may use the telephone (any time you wish).*	Вы мо́жете **воспо́льзоваться** телефо́ном. *You may use the telephone (at this moment).*

Considerations such as those above, however, affect only a small proportion of the cases in which мочь or similar expressions are used. Examination of any sample of the language will show that nine times out of ten they are followed by an infinitive in the perfective.

Живём мы, зна́ете, как на вулка́не . . . всё мо́жет **произойти́** . . .
We are living, you know, almost on a volcano . . . Anything may happen . . .

Он знал, что э́то глу́по, но всё-таки́ не мог **останови́ться.**
He knew that it was stupid, but all the same could not stop.

Ра́зве мы могли́ **вообрази́ть,** что тако́е а́томная бо́мба? (Э.)
Could we ever have imagined what the atomic bomb would be like?

Thus even where the statement has a general application the ˈendency is to focus attention rather on the fact that it is possible ɔr impossible) for the action in question to be brought to fruition.

Я никогда́ не смогу́ **поня́ть,** как же́нщина мо́жет жить с мужчи́ной, кото́рого не лю́бит. (Кон.)
I never will be able to understand how a woman can live with a man whom she does not love.

In this instance, of course, жить is the only possible choice as it ˈas no aspectival pair. Note, however, the perfective поня́ть even ˈfter the adverb никогда́, which explicitly makes the affirmation ˈood for all time. In the example which follows the influence has ˈen been sufficiently strong to induce the use of a perfective which ˈne would not have thought of as the natural choice in the context.

Вы мо́жете э́то **уви́деть** то́лько в Москве́.
You can see this only in Moscow. (Advertisement for the Bolshoi Ballet.)

ˈи́деть is more normally used for watching shows than уви́деть ˈhen referring to the past. Otherwise use смотре́ть/посмотре́ть.)

ˈ) **"It is Possible" etc.**

The expression мо́жно, whether used in the sense of "it is ˈossible" or "it is allowed", has also a strong tendency to take ˈe perfective infinitive. As has been noted above when, giving or ˈquesting permission it is normally found with the perfective

unless the permission is explicitly extended to a number of occa
sions.

Imperfective	Perfective
Мо́жно **входи́ть** к ним по ве- чера́м. *You can go in to them in the even- ings.*	Мо́жно **войти́?** *May I come in?*
Мо́жно **брать** э́ту кни́гу когда́ вам уго́дно. *You can take this book whenever you like.*	Мо́жно **взя́ть** э́ту кни́гу. *You can take this book (now).*

When used to express the simple concept of "possibility"
мо́жно often takes the perfective even in statements with a genera
application.

Мо́жно **привы́кнуть** ко всему́, так устро́ен челове́к. (Кон.)
*It is possible to get accustomed to everything; that is the way ma
is made.*

As with the verb мочь, мо́жно sometimes is followed by
perfective in cases where the imperfective would seem the mor
natural choice.

— Мо́жно **поду́мать,** что ты до́лжен знать про меня́ всё
(Кон.)
"*One might think that you ought to know all about me.*"

When considerations of "difficulty" or "process" intervene
мо́жно may be found with an imperfective.

— Как сейча́с лю́ди?
— Норма́льно. Мо́жно **закрыва́ть** связь.
— Да. Мне не́чего бо́льше сказа́ть тебе́. (Кон.)
"*How are the men now?*"
"*All right. You can close down contact.*"
"*Yes. I have nothing more to tell you.*"

The speaker has in mind the possible expenditure of time or energy involved in the actual process of breaking off wireless contact. закрыва́ть is a correct usage, but even in a case like this one, закры́ть would be more normally found.

Нельзя́ is the negative equivalent of мо́жно. In the sense of "it is impossible" it is followed by the perfective infinitive.

— Неуже́ли здесь нигде́ нельзя́ **доста́ть** такси́? (Кон.)
"Is it really impossible here to find a taxi anywhere?"

К сожале́нию, никогда́ нельзя́ **вспо́мнить** до конца́. (Акс.)
Unfortunately it is impossible to remember anything right through to the end.

On the other hand it should be remembered that when used in the sense of "it is forbidden", нельзя́ is normally found with the imperfective infinitive (see p. 118).

Corresponding to these two meanings of нельзя́ we find a similar differentiation made between the two aspects of the infinitive following не могу́ etc.

Imperfective	Perfective
Я не могу́ **переводи́ть** э́тот отры́вок. *I cannot translate this passage* (i.e. "I haven't time" or "I don't want to").	Я не могу́ **перевести́** э́тот отры́вок. *I cannot translate this passage* (i.e. "It is beyond my powers").
Я не могу́ **встава́ть.** *I cannot get up* (i.e. "The doctor has forbidden me to get up").	Я не могу́ **встать.** *I cannot get up* (i.e. "I have not the strength to get up" *or* "to stand up").
Я не могу́ **выходи́ть.** *I cannot go out* (i.e. "It is forbidden").	Я не могу́ **вы́йти.** *I cannot get out* (i.e. "I cannot open the door").

Another equivalent of нельзя́ with the perfective is found in expressions where the infinitive with a negative is used to express impossibility.

Как она́ стара́! . . . Уж никогда́ — никогда́ не **вы́прямить** э́тот со́гнутый стан и ста́вшую кру́глой уже́ спи́ну, не **истончи́ть** грома́дные набря́кшие но́ги, не **согре́ть** холо́дные ру́ки. (Казв.)
How old she is! . . . Never, never again will it be possible to straighten that bent waist and her back which is already curved, to make slender again her huge flabby legs, or to warm her cold hands.

(c) " To Manage to"

Naturally there is an even stronger call for the perfective infinitive in cases where it is clearly stated that a given action has been brought to a successful conclusion.

В мо́лодости мне удало́сь два́жды **побыва́ть** в Ита́лии. (Э.)
In my youth I managed to visit Italy twice.

An imperfective infinitive could not be substituted here unless the main verb were also in the imperfective (удава́лось.) The introduction of a negative has no influence on the aspect of the infinitive.

Каю́ту не удало́сь **отвоева́ть.** Придётся е́хать в тре́тьем кла́ссе. (Вор.)
We have not managed to win a cabin. We will have to travel in the third class.
Убежа́ть удава́лось не всегда́. (Ильф.)
They did not always succeed in getting away.

The verb успе́ть in contemporary Russian is restricted to this sense of "limited time" in which a given action must be completed.

Шофёр успе́л **заме́длить** ход. (Ол.)
The driver had time to slow down.
Но не успе́л Во́ва Большо́й **собра́ть** кома́нду. (Гла.)
But " Big" Vova had not time to collect his team.

As in the case of мочь, успе́ть often induces a rather unexpected perfective.

— Ну и пе́кло. Не успе́ешь **написа́ть,** черни́ла со́хнут. (Ант.)
"*It was baking hot. You had not time to write before the ink dried up.*"
... за мо́лодость, кото́рую я не успе́л **уви́деть** ... (Ол.)
... *for youth which I had not time to see* ...

In this example the underlying meaning is that the speaker had not time "to glimpse" his youth as it flashed by. The length of time over which the action extends is quite immaterial; what is stressed is the fact that it has been brought to a conclusion.

— Чем она́ занима́ется?
— Она́ мно́гим успе́ла **позанима́ться.** Око́нчила ку́рсы иностра́нных языко́в, рабо́тала официа́нткой в како́м-то Интури́стком заведе́нии, пото́м перево́дчицей в само́м «Интури́сте».
"*What is her job?*"
"*She has managed to fit in a lot of things. She finished the foreign language courses, worked as waitress in some place under Intourist and then as an interpreter for Intourist itself.*"

When the imperfective успева́ть is introduced there is often an option of using either aspect in the infinitive.

Он успева́л ка́ждый раз **приходи́ть/прийти́** во́время.
He managed to arrive in time on every occasion.

(d) Miscellaneous

The *Grammatika russkogo yazyka* lists the following verbs as being used invariably with perfectives:

ожида́ть: *to expect*
умудри́ться: *to succeed* (lit. *to have sufficient cunning to.*)

With some other verbs such as сметь/посме́ть the infinitive tends to reflect the aspect of the auxiliary.

Он смел меня́ **упрека́ть.**
Он посме́л меня́ **упрекну́ть.**
He dared to reproach me.

This is not however a rule with universal application.

(3) Necessity

(a) Obligation

The perfective infinitive is found after words such as до́лжен, ну́жно, whether they convey the idea of an imposed necessity or a duty.

Он до́лжен был **произнести́** речь.
He had to deliver a speech .

Вам **доплати́ть** четы́ре копе́йки.
You have to pay a further four kopecks.

Вы же сказа́ли о своём бра́те, что его́ на́до **расстреля́ть.** (Ол.)
You said of your brother that he ought to be shot.

Оста́лась то́лько ле́стница. Я слы́шу уже́ голоса́. Оста́лось **одоле́ть** то́лько не́сколько ступе́нек. (Ол.)
Only the stairs remain. I can already hear voices. All I have to do is to get up a few steps.

Потре́бовалось ему́ заче́м-то во вре́мя хо́да **перебра́ться** с головно́й дво́йки на после́днюю па́ру. (Вор.)
He had for some reason or other to get across from the leading pair onto the last pair (of boats) while they were moving along . . .

Only in rare cases, where continuous or repetitive concepts occur, is the imperfective used.

Мы обеспе́чили себе́ веду́щее положе́ние и мы должны́ **сохраня́ть** его́.

We have secured a leading position for ourselves and we must maintain it.

Мне прихо́дится ка́ждый раз **поправля́ть** его́.

I have to correct him every time.

(b) Advice

As a counterpart to expressions of "dissuasion" (noted on pp. 117–121) expressions containing positive advice will naturally tend to have perfective infinitives,

Са́мое ве́рное в таки́х слу́чаях — бы́стро **встать** и **заня́ться** де́лом. (Вор.)

The safest thing in such circumstances is to stand up quickly and get on with your work.

Similarly, as the opposite to не сто́ит with the imperfective we find сто́ит with perfectives.

Но сто́ит лишь **перевести́** взгляд на бе́рег, как сра́зу ста́нет я́сно . . . (Вор.)

It is only a question of looking round at the bank when it will immediately become obvious . . .

Lastly we may notice an interesting distinction between the shades of meaning conveyed by substituting one aspect of the infinitive for the other after the word пора́.

Imperfective	Perfective
Пора́ **уезжа́ть.**	Пора́ **уе́хать.**
It is time we were going.	*It is high time we were gone.*

Пото́м он стал ду́мать, что пора́ бы ему́ **перебра́ться** в го́род, **поступи́ть** куда́-нибудь учи́ться. (Кон.)

Then he began to think that it was high time he moved into town and entered some institute to study.

In practice, because of considerations of courtesy пора́ is most frequently encountered with an imperfective infinitive.

Index to Verbs

Aspectival pairs are not given in this index. Only verbs which are commented on are included. For key to letters and numbers see contents. In order to avoid confusion verbs mentioned in the introduction have been listed under G for "general".

List of authors quoted

Bibliography

1. О. С. Ахманова: Очерки по общей и русской лексикологии, Учпедгиз, Москва, 1957.
2. Л. А. Булаховский: Курс русского литературного языка, Харьков, 1937.
3. ред. В. В. Виноградов: Грамматика русского языка, Издательство Академии наук, Москва, 1960, 3 т.
4. ред. В. В. Виноградов: Современный русский язык, Издательство московского университета, Москва, 1952.
5. А. В. Исаченко: Грамматический строй русского языка в сопоставлении с словацким, том II, Издательство словацкой академии наук, Братислава, 1960.
6. ред. П. С. Кузнецов и др.: Русский язык для студентов-иностранцев, Госиздат «Советская наука», Москва, 1957, 1959, 1960.
7. И. М. Пулькина: Краткий справочник по русской грамматике, Учпедгиз, Москва, 1961.
8. А. И. Смирницкий: Морфология английского языка, Издательство литературы на иностранных языках, Москва, 1959.
9. А. А. Спагис: Образование и употребление видов глагола в русском языке, Учпедгиз, Москва, 1961.
10. F. F. Borras and R. F. Christian: *Russian Syntax*, Oxford University Press, 1959.
11. D. P. Costello: Tenses in Indirect Speech in Russian, *Slavonic and East European Review*, London, June 1961.
12. J. Ferrell: On the aspects of *byt'* and on the Position of the Periphrastic Imperfective Future in Contemporary Literary Russian, *Word*, vol. IX, no. 4, New York, 1953.

13. A. Mazon: *Emploi des aspects du verbe russe*, Edouard Champion, Paris, 1914.
14. L. Stilman: *Russian verbs of motion*, King's Crown Press, New York, 1951.
15. W. F. Tulasiewicz: A Lesson on the Aspects of the Verb in Russian, *Modern Language Journal*, no. 8, Buffalo–St. Louis, 1962.